Subtle Secrets

TALKING HEART TO HEART

"You are fired." said the Heart to the Ego. "You have been measured, you have been weighed, judged and you have been found wanting."

Ed Rychkun

Editing: Hope Rychkun
Cover design: Manoj Sharma
www.indyahub.com

ISBN 978-0-9782623-4-1

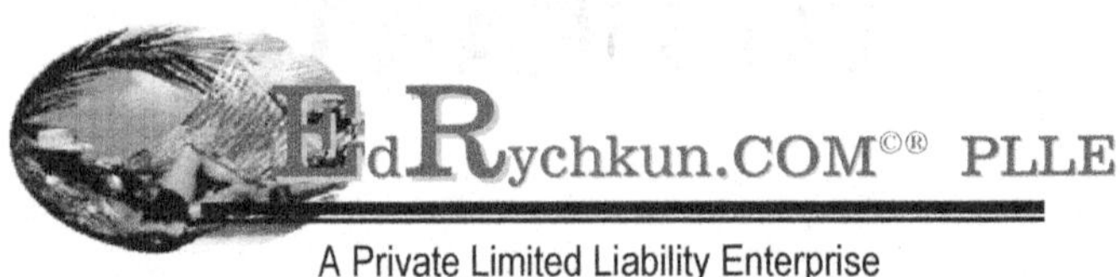

A Private Limited Liability Enterprise

CONTENTS

A SPECIAL DEDICATION

This little book is dedicated to my sons **Sterling** and **Shane Rychkun**. When I look back at all of the different paths my life took, I recall a complex patchwork of different people I have loved and met, things I have seen, and events that made up my life's dramas and joys. I cannot but think about how I perceived these then and now. While sometimes I felt like I had entered a Hell on earth, other times I felt like I had found Heaven. Now, upon reflection, I think back to one previous time where one of the most difficult choices came about when my path split. The path I perceived as the right one created a disruption in compassion and love towards my two sons whom I lost for a time along that journey. I found my Soul Mate on that path but during a critical time in my son's lives, I was not there and that loss stalked deep in my subconscious eventually leading to the manifestation of this book. It was on this path that I found pieces of wisdom that allowed me to understand why my life was as it was. It is to them I dedicate the most valued knowledge that I came upon as a result of my life lessons – and the secrets of creating a peaceful, joyful, and prosperous life. This book is my Genie in the lamp and it is my wish that this knowledge becomes their Genie as well.

Ed Rychkun

DO YOU HAVE ENOUGH QUALITY TIME?

Have you ever wondered where the expressions "from the bottom of my heart", "heartless" or "heart of gold" come from and what the heart has to do with the saying? We use these terms as being meaningful but without realizing exactly what the reason is. The heart is just another organ in the body. Why not say "from the bottom of my liver"? Well, would you believe the expressions actually relate to your prime purpose in life and the process by which the subtle energies between your heart energy center and your mind, body and spirit operate? The heart is the area where your core being exists. Life is a miracle gifted to you so you could use free choice to experience love and compassion – that is a prime purpose of the "heart." The choice of how to experience events you draw to you define the degree of quality in your life. Your life has turned out to be the way it is because of the way you have worked with the subtle energy systems connecting you to the universe – that is also related to the "heart." Yes, the heart does a lot more than you think.

So this is why I want to talk to you in a "Heart to Heart" manner. This mode of expression is one that carries emotion of compassion and concern – genuine feelings. I hope what I am about to talk to you about can improve the quality of your life as it has mine. There are four central themes to what this talk is about. The first is that we are all connected – one family so to speak — for a purpose of love, peace and abundance. The second is that you can control the extent and degree of quality in your life. The third is that if you want to have a peaceful planet then you must first have peace with yourself. The fourth is that your life is a reflection of how you work with the *Subtle Laws of the Universe*. Now, these four statements at first glance may not appear to be profound but when you begin to understand how these subtle laws of the Universe actually work, and how they have dealt you the quality of life you have, they will become profound revelations. Then you will be in a position to completely change the quality of your life on this planet.

But first, I need to ask you some questions – the ones that used to perplex me. Do you **believe** that the events in your life are there because you have drawn them to you? And further, do you **believe** that what you choose to do with these is entirely up to you? Do you **believe** that what you resist will continue to persist? Do you **believe** you have the power to manifest quality time – and anything else you want, including miracles? The answers are all YES. Of particular importance is the last question. The first key to actually manifesting quality time resides in the word **believe**. This is the roadblock that prevents you from properly answering yes to these questions. You may ask: WHY SHOULD I BELIEVE THIS? Fair enough. This means that you may need some new convincing information for your belief system. I am going to present you with the Subtle Laws of the Universe in a very concise form. Then, assuming you realize the correlation with your current life, the big question will become HOW? HOW can I actually manifest a life full of quality time? I am going to tell you exactly how in a simple daily routine.

Now, let us pursue the notion of quality time because it has a different meaning to every individual. How much time do you have in a day that is truly QUALITY TIME? I mean REAL quality time as a result of some GREAT EXPERIENCE. What is it? Can you define it? To me it is time resulting from some experience that really makes me — my mind, body and soul — **FEEL GOOD**. I mean REALLY good! So, here is the big question: What would you write down as the most meaningful, important quality time you have had? If you did this, would you list three components — physical, emotional and spiritual **feelings** associated with that time?

The definition of what quality time is to you, and what feelings go with the time is a crucial notion to understanding how things can work to your favor. The three components of physical (**Body**), emotional (**Mind**) and soul (**Spirit)** were designed to produce FEELINGS that work in harmony. What are the feelings? Let me use an example. You are in love with someone and you meet for a date. When you first see each other, there is an immediate thought coming from the mind as you trigger an emotional feeling. You think: *"This is really great, I like this. It makes me feel good."* Then your physical body does its own thing to generate a physical feeling. Your heartbeat rises, you may get tingles and the body gets excited because it also feels. Then your soul has its own feelings, perhaps more difficult to identify. You exude a feeling of completeness and peace emanating from your "heart." It is something unexplainable that stirs deep inside of you – from the *"bottom of your heart."* Why is it important to define these three levels? Well, there are many more things happening inside and around you than you are aware of. They make up your complete essence and the greatest moments of quality time are when these three are synchronized in harmony. This is the "technology" of your Trinity (Body, Mind and Spirit) governed by the subtle laws of energy.

Now I have to explain briefly why I refer to these laws as "subtle." The best way to relate to this is to consider a wireless versus hardwire system of communication. The brain-nervous system in our bodies is a hardwire system sending and receiving electrical impulses back and forth. But we have another invisible system composed of energy centers with invisible lines of wireless communication connecting to the wire system and out into the rest of the universe. It is the subtle system. It works away dealing with energy packets and signals unbeknown to us because science has not considered this minute system (hence subtle) of energy movement of any significance. So the energies and communications

work away on autopilot because we have never considered them to be available to pilot. Even worse is that we are influencing them dramatically without knowing it. Although "science" and "medicine" are rapidly changing their ideas about these subtle centers, they have been DEAD WRONG about their importance. The tip of the iceberg is the hardwire side. The bottom of the iceberg is the wireless side — the one that receives input from the Universe, our environment, our body, mind and spirit. And the greatest "sleeper" in all this is how this invisible wireless network is controlled by the mind and the energies of emotion. They follow specific laws of behavior to indirectly and directly reflect your degree of health, wealth and quality time – as you are about to understand.

So how can one create more quality time? Understand and pay more attention to how these laws work. Harmonize with the Prime Purpose and Process of subtle energies. Everybody has quality time resulting from a diversity of experiences. It is noteworthy that quality time is not related to negative experiences that create the emotions of fear, anger, hatred, stress, anxiety, conflict or the likes. These in fact block quality time as they set up destructive "harmonics" in your body — as you will find out shortly. Rather, quality times are most often a result of experiences that create positive emotions of love, peace, reverence, compassion, joy, forgiveness, and gratitude. So if there is an imbalance in your life where you are on the treadmill constantly trying to keep moving, living the dramas of business, money, banks, relationships, regulations, bills, and the negativity dominant in the media, these are creating experiences where fear, anxiety, stress, and discord are your norm. These create harmonics that are destructive resulting in three problems; they end up manifesting into body, mind and spirit dysfunction; they end up manifesting more of the same experiences; they end up stopping your spiritual growth — your and everyone else's purpose in life.

There is another critical notion stuck deep in these problems. If you want to see a peaceful planet with no conflict, full of love and peace, then you must first start with placing these in YOUR OWN life. Love yourself and be at peace with yourself FIRST. This, as you will find out, is because of the way the subtle laws work. What you believe and feel — your consciousness — is reflected directly in a whole planetary consciousness. Hard to believe? Decide for yourself after reading the laws. This is a short book designed to get to the point. As a former scientist and businessman, my quest for answers started in science but they were not found there. They were obscure pieces of a puzzle found in ancient writings, esoteric material, ancient traditions, prophesies, religious beliefs, the New Age belief system, science and even the bible. This in itself brings a huge resounding message to all on the planet because the resulting conclusions about the Laws transcend all races, creeds, religions, beliefs, and cultures. The message here should be clear. We all should be focused on the underlying common denominator of a universal goal of peace and abundance. Yes, there are common denominators in all of this. I rationalized them into these Secret Subtle Laws of the Universe. Why are they secret? I have no intention in explaining except to say it is because they have either been deleted from public information, obscured in ancient writings, ignored by science, or kept to a secret segment of mankind. What does this all suggest? We are all after the same thing — a quality life full of love, abundance and peace. Once you strip the conflicts and differences out of all of the material, the answers are simple common denominators because ALL races state love, family, joy and happiness are what life is all about. Well, if we are all part of one cosmic family seeking the same purpose, the answers being the same for all, why do we need to fight over differences on how to get to the same spot? At the bottom of the illusion of conflict, there are no differences? We will revisit this at the end of the book as I believe by then you will clearly understand this.

My quest for answers to questions about how the universe worked, who I was, what I was here for led me to a lot of different information pathways. At the root of this was my need to find the answer to the fundamental questions: **Why is my life the way it is?** and **How can I manifest a better quality life?** Where did the answers come from? As I said above, it was bits and pieces from ancient prophesies, old cultures, old religious information, new religious findings, spiritual information, the New Age material, what science has discovered about cosmic workings, and a place I never expected to find anything — inside ME.

This little booklet is my summary of what I deemed as relevant to proactively creating a better life. This is what I mean when I use the term manifesting. It means that I manifest a desired experience — I co-create it. I am not going to spend much space attempting to prove or justify what I am going to tell you. I have written a lot of books on the topic and these are listed at the back of this book. These are placed there if you want details and references. I think that as you read the laws and how to apply them you will begin to relate them to your past and current life. You should begin to correlate the laws with why your life is the way it is. That will be your "scientific" proof which will change your mind — that is crucial — about how you can go forward in a better light. Once you "see the light" and understand how these laws have been working *against you*, the process of changing things to have the laws work *for you* should be clear. I am then going to present you with the steps to do this. Then the rest is up to you and only you.

HAVE A LOOK AT YOUR LIFE

Before we get into the Laws, let us try to encapsulate where we are now. There are two life movies being played out – yours and the planets. Let us stop the action on these movies for a minute. There appears to be a serious dis-ease, a serious virus everywhere. That virus is that we are not getting our share of prosperity. We are not having enough abundance and joy. Our bodies are not taking the wear and tear well enough. Something is obviously not right. The New Age beliefs say prosperity, abundance and joy are our birthright. In fact, if you are able to *"read between the lines"* of obscurity you find that religions and ancient wisdom also say the same. All we do is believe and take it. This is a prevalent belief everywhere. Well, HELLO, is anybody paying attention here? What Birthright? Believe what? Take it how? It doesn't take a genius to see the planet is heavily laden with war, conflict, sick, poor, helpless, angry people that are quite obviously not getting their "fair share" of abundance, joy and prosperity. Why? What should be is NOT what is.

If you look into this conundrum more deeply, in bibles, religions, ancient writings, esoteric sciences, etc., etc., you find a lot of obscurity on why this is so. Then you find a lot of people who obviously can't "walk the talk." Well, it is said, there are things you haven't *"figured out yet"* or you need to *"hire an expert."* There are also a lot of conflicting, uncorrelated materials that do not lead to an answer. But in this quagmire, the New Age is most direct on answering this conundrum. It tells us that our abilities to take our fair share of abundance and joy have eluded us and that the emotions of fear, anger and hate have atrophied our ability to manifest it. Our minds and bodies are not functioning at full capacity. Money and differences in beliefs have contributed to hostility, fear, anger, wars, poverty and destruction — all blocking our abilities. The root, they say is due to our belief of duality (being separate from Spirit) contributing to judgment, power, competition and our need to feed our greed for material gratification — the Ego. We are too negative and Egotistical — trying to simply survive. It paints a pretty dismal picture of a species out of balance — weighted to the negative dark side. So? Does this have any impact on our quality time and our ability to manifest it? Does the intensity of negative reactions, opinions and beliefs have any impact on your life? Think about it. Are you driven by your Ego or by your heart? Does your Ego EVER get satisfied? Is it then a stretch to comprehend that a negative out-of-balance human is not going to have an abundance of quality time?

The New Age, ancient wisdom and religions all say we need to love our neighbors a bit more than we have been. Considering the last century has killed some hundred million people because of "differences", that's an understatement! And then there are our bodies. We have effectively poisoned these with toxins and horrible pollutants that have made us fat, sick and lazy. We are physically and mentally dysfunctional. That's NOT an understatement! We are always fearful of something — debt, bills, loss, lawyers, terrorists, tax collectors, regulations, death, sickness, it never ends. And we are always drumming to bankers, money, bosses, the system, listening to the bad news channels and reading the negative murders, theft, rape, corruption, sickness headlines in the newspapers. Our Egos drive us to get more, protect our pride better — more, better, more. That, the New Age says, is NOT the right medicine to fix the dysfunction. So even our bodies — the machinery to create quality time — are in dire need of repair.

From this scenario, one could deduct that the prognosis doesn't look so good for a lot of people. The chances for recovery are not the best. We have a dysfunctional body, sluggish mind and obviously what we believe doesn't seem to work. In the meantime, life's treadmill goes on and on stuck like a broken record playing the same tune. Clearly, if fear and negative feelings are a reflection of life, something has to change. If there are indeed subtle laws we are not aware of that are working away creating this "un-quality" time, then we have unknowingly become MASTERS in using the laws!

Well, that is exactly what we have done. WE have through a lack of understanding of these laws mirrored a personal life and a planetary life reflecting EXACTLY what we have asked for — a negative, dysfunctional mass of people. That is what we have individually and jointly manifested. So why can't we switch this around? WE CAN! What must change first, however, is your belief in yourself and a belief that such a change is readily within your grasp. It starts with YOU. But first, YOU need to understand what the laws are and how they work. Then you need to get your equipment OFF autopilot onto a more proactive plan.

So now I have to stop preaching and tell you about the **Secret Subtle Laws of the Universe**. These laws have been extracted from many sources and my "inner self." When you read them, you may say that you already knew some. Whether you do or not doesn't matter. What you believe and follow going forward in a daily routine, however, does. The depth of conviction to the belief and its deployment is up to you. It is like learning anything in life. The more you imbed in your belief system, the more you dedicate yourself to what you learn, the better are the results. As you are about to find out, you are already manifesting what your life is now. You probably did not realize how. The expressions *"What you visualize you materialize"* and *"Energy flows where attention goes"* will shortly ring clearly, even though you may not be aware of it. In this respect, think about your typical day and how many times you think negative thoughts, use negative words, feel anger or fear, compete, judge, fight about something, and simply let your Ego drive your desires.

When you finish reading the Laws, you will wonder how they are actually deployed in your personal life to be effective for you. I have said this before but it is important that you and your life be the proof to you. The first real "revelation" will come to you when you begin to understand how these laws have already been working diligently, under *your* command, and *on autopilot* to create the kind of life you already have. Once that awareness hits you, you will be able to understand how important it is to start a new strategy to change your life as you move forward.

Once you realize this, you will ask how do I use these in my everyday life to create a new future and more quality time. Some of you, I am certain, are already doing it and you will confirm the laws. The answer lies in a complete body, mind and spirit plan that respects the Laws. When you were created, given the "spark of life", and took your first breath of air, you were given control of a very sophisticated bio-computer that operates on information coming from subtle and non-subtle places. These places create minute energy fields behaving to their own rhythms and laws. The bio-computer is preprogrammed when the life force and first breath activated it. It is programmed to perform certain functions on auto-pilot and pilot. It is always working as it receives input instructions from you, your mind, your words and emotions, the environment and its internal monitoring systems. It is fully integrated and is designed to respond to the Body, Mind and Spirit with the mind as the interactive software programmer. When the three components are not working together, the input and the output get garbled and you say hello to dysfunction and dis-ease. The Laws that I am going to tell you about will reveal how this bio-computer works in conjunction with a much larger computer — like the Internet — the Big Guy in the sky, or that larger computer I refer to as the Universal Mind (Spirit).

You need to know why I keep referring to the Subtle Laws as "LAWS." They behave in a predictable manner like the laws of gravity or magnetism. In further laying out the process of earthly behavior in such a way as to work WITH these laws, I call that the CODE OF LIFE. Why? Because the process sets the Code. This is the computer program instruction set that runs your bio-computer, your life and determines the quality of the output you receive. I think the easiest way to grasp this is to look at a symphony orchestra and a conductor as an analogy. You — namely your mind — are the rightful conductor. The orchestra is made up of various instrumental sections that need to play a complete piece of music. First, they can play some classical piece, or they can play rock. As an aside, you will learn that soft harmonic classical music has a soothing effect of peace on people while rock music has an effect of creating anger and hostility. So you as the conductor of this orchestra need to first decide the piece of music to play, then make sure you practice enough to keep all of the different sections in harmony playing the same tune. If you play a nice piece, your audience will be happy, in harmony and peace as they listen. If you do a poor job, they will become irritated, angry and even leave. Well, your body has these various instrumental sections that also need direction. Your body is vibrating like musical notes with different instrumental sections having specific frequencies to contribute to the piece you choose to play. These sections are the subtle energy centers (brain, heart, chakras to name a few) each responsible for different instruments and processes that need to be synchronized into the playing the right music in harmony. If these are in harmony, the audience (trillions of cells) picking up the resulting harmonics through the subtle fields and body antenna (nerves) work together in harmony to optimize the functionality of the body. If not, they fall into discord, which over time will gravitate to a self-fulfilling cycle of stress, health and poor well being — dysfunction. It will impact your body, mind and amount of quality time. Now, unbeknown to you, this orchestra — via the Ego — has been deciding what tune to play and how to play it. So as an orchestra conductor, you need to take charge to change this picture.

THE SECRET SUBTLE LAWS OF THE UNIVERSE

The following laws reflect the subtle workings of the Universe with you at the center. Of particular importance is that these laws reflect how your body, mind and spirit relate to the rest of the Universe. You are now clear that *subtle* refers to minute energies, currents and processes that are normally undetectable and invisible. If one could use examples from our materialistic science world, these would be gravity, magnetism, electromagnetism, photons, radiation, microwave, and ultraviolet energies. We are all aware of these energy forces and what they do to us and our environment. But there are more subtle, less conspicuous, less "scientifically" measurable energies that are busily working away quietly in accordance with their own set laws that we do not pay a lot of attention to. These are vibrational energies that have to do with a cosmic purpose, thoughts, words, and emotion. They use minute lines of force creating communication between body, mind and spirit to the rest of the universe.

The truth is that these subtle energies, and the laws surrounding the way they work have always been around us. And you have already been using these laws more than you could ever believe. What you want to put into a new belief system is this: they exist, they affect your life, and if you have NOT been in harmony with them you have not been controlling your share of quality time as much as you could. It is the awareness of these laws and the method of deployment that is the key to optimizing the joys in your life.

Science, ancient wisdom, esoterics, religions, particularly Eastern, and Agers have converged on the topic of a Divine force or Creator. There is a Divine Intelligence working with the Individual (your) Intelligence. To name some of the heavy players at your (individual) level there are three players taking up the lion's share of subtle energy manipulators. These are the brain, the heart and the chakras. The old players now understood better are the seven major energy centers (chakras). The brain has always been known to be the big controller but the heart is the new kid on the block. These take orders from subtle energies and work away with their own invisible communication channels inside and outside the body, interconnecting us with information coming from the universe and our immediate material world. These are receiving and transmitting information constantly, either automatically or with our "added" information.

As you read through the Laws which follow, be cognizant of the fact that everything — yes EVERYTHING — is energy. This means that thoughts, words and emotions are all energy. Then the other notion is that the "Great Nothing" of space, between atoms, between what we perceive as "solid" account for 95% of all that exists. This "nothing' has now been shown to have intelligence, purpose and behavior. This phenomenon is commonly referred to as Spirit, Divine Intelligence, The Force, God, The Ether, The Creator, and many other names. Whatever your name for it is, it is the "spiritual glue" that makes everything work. I am going to refer to this as "Spirit" but the name is not significant. The existence of a FORCE which has purpose and laws, however, is.

In a nutshell, the basic question for you is whether you are in harmony with life's purpose and how "aligned" you are with the subtle energies and natural forces. If you are out of harmony, then it becomes more difficult to grow (ascend) the spiritual side. You will be affecting the body by creating more stress and anxiety — which will eventually manifest more dis-ease and dysfunction than you want. The most revealing point to this is that the more aligned, and in harmony you are, the easier it becomes to manifest what you want. The laws are of two groups. The first two reflect PURPOSE. The others reflect PROCESS. Are you ready? Read these slowly.

THE LAW OF ASCENSION

We are here on this planet to evolve our consciousness until it becomes One with the light which created it. We, as part of Spirit (Light) are here to see the glory of all that is. All that is — everything, yes everything — is energy in a state of vibration. We also vibrate. Evolving our consciousness is synonymous with the process of raising our vibrations. Our purpose is to understand who we really are by learning from our experiences. When vibrations rise in us, this is referred to as ascension. This process, when raised like a thermometer beyond a threshold, allows us to remember our true lineage and our connection to a higher power, or "Spirit" which we are part of. This Spirit has many names but it is the same regardless of race, religion or practice (God, Divine Intelligence, Cosmic Mind, Lord, Jesus, etc.). We are born here with our bodies, minds and spirit working in a low end vibrational energy state referred to as 3D (physical being). The lower, or slower the vibrations are, the more solid is the appearance of the vibrating matter. A rock has very slow vibrations! The process of ascending matter in the 3D material world requires a specific type of energy "furnace" to raise vibrations. For example putting the energy of fire under solid ice drives the electrons to vibrate faster (higher) and the solid changes its energy form from solid ice, to liquid, to gas, then pure spiritual energy – its original state. Each energy state exhibits newly activated energy forms and properties which do not become apparent until a specific level of vibration is reached. Any material object can be transformed this way by the use of fire. In fact, we could also transform this way into pure spiritual energy, as when death occurs and your Spirit goes Home to the Big Spirit in the Sky, but there is a much better energy furnace available to us.

We are made up of body, mind and spirit. The mind is the bridge between body and spirit. There are three main components to the mind, namely the Higher Self

(Spirit), the Lower Self (Ego) and your individual mind which bridges the other two. We are designed with energy centers called chakras that control the body's subtle energy fields. These invisible centers vibrate in unison with the bodies surrounding subtle electromagnetic fields, communicating between universal energies and body functions (as noted in the field of acupuncture). Each center has specific purposes and capabilities. The higher centers (top three chakras) have capabilities (Spiritual) that cannot be activated or their true properties deployed until we rise to a certain vibratory level as fueled by a specific energy force through ascension. The strongest positive energy forces that do this are love and compassion. Once higher energy centers are activated as ascension progresses we change from our 3D form to 4D (hyper being) and then ultimately to a 5D (spiritual light being). In the 3D state, we are used to the five sensory world of taste, smell, feel, sight, and hearing but there are many more abilities – and more enhanced states that we cannot develop until they become operational, or liberated through higher vibration. As vibrations rise, the range of existing sensory systems expands so you see, hear, feel, smell and taste beyond the normal frequency ranges.

As ascension progresses, new Spiritual abilities become possible, some examples being mental projection, psychic/distance healing, clairvoyance, clairaudience, clairsentience, precognition, telepathy, channeling, telekinesis, psycho kinesis, psychommetry, bilocation, levitation, time travel, teleportation, and so on. This set of new abilities and capabilities expands with the ascension process until you reach the ultimate vibratory state of pure spiritual energy, just as water does when fuelled by fire. So your body needs to grow and be nourished to develop properly, as does your spirit need to grow and develop. The link between the two, the mind, has this responsibility.

THE LAW OF LOVE

Coupled tightly to the Law of Ascension is the energy force of love. It is the vibrational energy engine, the true power in the Universe. This force has a natural purpose to create a positive harmony based on Love. Clearly, without it, life on this planet would have perished long ago. It is the universal energy force upon which all life's purpose was designed. As light grows other organisms (like plants), love is required to "grow" the spiritual side of a human. Life is a miracle gifted to you so you could use free choice to experience love and compassion. The choice of how to experience events you draw to you define the degree of quality in your life. Our purpose is to learn how to convert all we experience to be in harmony with the natural law of Love. Unconditional Love, when charged emotionally by a human, is a potent energy force recognized by Spirit. The more love you generate, the higher are your vibrations. The force of love harmonizes and creates a coherent energy wave feeding the ascension stages, as do other love based emotions. The opposite negative (dark) emotions based on fear and anger are energy disruptors that stop the ascension engine and descends the vibrations.

There is no distinction between you, an atom, a thing, the universe or Spirit. The rotating Universe is like a nucleus with rotating electrons. Everything functions (vibrates) through a vitalization of electrons by the life force, natural laws and the underlying force of love, forming a hologram. As you fill your consciousness (mind) and body with love, you contribute to the cosmic consciousness, lifting vibrations of the planet, making it a better place to live, reap abundance, joy and prosperity. As you open up to new abilities that are synchronized with these higher vibrations, you are able to co-create your desires faster and you evolve towards your Divine nature, leaving the importance of the material world behind. Your Divine nature, your ability to give unconditional love, and reap peace, joy and abundance is your birthright.

THE LAW OF COSMIC INTELLIGENCE

Science has confirmed that a "cosmic intelligence" exists everywhere, has been here eternally, and has an intelligent response system. It is within us and outside of us throughout the total universe. It is a universal communication medium referred to as the ether, nothing, Divine Matrix, Universal Spirit, the something that science has traditionally said was nothing but empty space. This makes up some 95% of everything that exists. Is not empty space. It is a living medium. Science has said we use only 10% of our brain. We have not developed the rest that connects with that living medium. Science says we use only two of the twelve DNA strands. They are part of the living medium which is holographic. That living, conscious, intelligent medium is what keeps what we believe to have form and life functioning, spinning, moving and "alive." Our minds are also "nothing" definable that are part of the universal medium communicating through the subtle energies. What is the essence of this medium and its intelligence? God, Creator, the Force, whatever you want to call it. I refer to it as Spirit and the Universal Mind. We communicate with Spirit through words, thoughts, feelings and emotion. These constitute the language or technology of communication that we use either directly or indirectly.

We have an individual mind, consciousness and intelligence with a library of all that we have experienced. So does Spirit have the same Universal Mind, consciousness and intelligence with a library (Akasic) of all that was or is. Our mind is not part of our physical body and resides in the local aura, which in turn links with the Universal Mind. Do you remember the Borg in Star Trek? The Universal Mind responds to emotion in a holographic way in that each piece is a mirror of the whole. A change in one piece mirrors through the whole. That is the way it is designed. In this way, our mind, or our local consciousness holding our beliefs, thoughts, emotions and experiences are reflected in the "whole" — the Universal Mind. It is therefore a mirror of our combined global consciousness. So as our individual lives are a reflection of our consciousness (beliefs, energies and actions), so is the global (planetary) consciousness a result of composite beliefs, energies and actions. At the minute level, our DNA is an integral part of the Universal holographic Mind, the other ten "useless" strands being our connection to the rest of the Universal Mind and to Spirit.

At lower levels of being, there is a third or local mind (group) which is best illustrated when birds in a flock move together instantaneously because their minds (hence brain controlling physical flight) are functioning as one mind. This is the way DNA is designed, each of the billions of cells being encoded as the whole — so any one cell can create a whole human and when one is changed, all others are also changed instantly regardless of distance, also being holographic. In the example of birds, not only is the individual DNA upgraded when a new survival tactic is learned, but at some critical threshold where several birds learn the same new tactic, the rest of the same species DNA becomes "upgraded" thereby adding to the survival abilities of the species — called instinct. What is the threshold that modifies the DNA code in a local or global consciousness? Science has shown that the square root of 1% of the population is all it takes to change the whole. That amount of "same consciousness" in a group (DNA) will reflect itself through the whole consciousness (DNA), regardless of distance! Our minds are therefore linked to the Universal Mind and as vibrations increase (ascension) the abilities to connect, access and understand Spirit increases.

THE LAW OF COMMUNICATION

The communication system, or language, serving the first two laws of purpose operate with Universal and individual minds according to specific processes. As everything is made of vibrating energy, communication behaves according to particular unique natural laws encompassing energy movement and minute subtle lines of force. Of particular importance here is the energy created and further "energized" by a human. These energies include thoughts, emotion, words, objects, pictures, visualizations, and other such things that we create or use in our regular activities but have paid little attention to. They vibrate at their own specific frequencies and have unique characteristics. These energies operate under a law of attraction that is designed to seek out or draw like energy to them. The energy forms into "packets" which once created and projected, seek out other packets in the form of events, people, thoughts, ideas and so on that will contribute to the manifestation of what the particular energy represents. The Universal Mind will simply mirror back as best it can what the packet reflects. As a result, *"what you think about, you bring about"* and *"energy flows where your attention goes"* are critical notions to *always* be aware of. What is crucial to this notion is that we are designed to always be manifesting energy packets and that the energy creation process does not care whether it is dark (bad) or light (good) energy. This process is happening automatically whether you know it or not. You have no idea when you will attract or manifest the results but your mind and the Universal Mind will work towards finding the appropriate energies to give you the desired experience. The speed of the manifestation process depends on the strength of the energy and clarity of the focus you place on the packet.

Think about how gravity or magnetism work. Invisible force lines pull or repel specific things. The law of attraction pulls like energy packets (vibrations) closer. If the thoughts are fragmented, the power of the energy to manifest anything is weak. Needless to say, the strength or intensity of the thoughts (focus) is key to the speed of the manifestation. The process of manifestation involves converting a thought (*I think it would be nice to have a drink*) to an intent (*I need to get up walk over to the fridge*) to an action (*get up and get a beer*) to manifestation (*drinking the beer*). This is obvious but a thought like *"I would like to have a million dollars"* which may not be totally under your control, requires the Universal Mind to assist you in manifesting the million dollars. There are three ways to accelerate this process. The first is to focus on being in harmony with the universal purpose so you can ascend and invoke new powers to manifest things faster. The second is to create a field of total harmony with the Subtle laws to maximize their force and your power. The third is to make your desires strong positive visualizations that are further fueled by strong, positive mind and body feelings.

In further expanding on communications with regards to letters, words, sentences, and thoughts, you need to be aware that these are energies that are projected varying in strength. They carry with them qualities that are further energized by human emotion. Just think for a moment what happens to your mind and body when someone screams "fire", or when you pick up the phone and the caller says he is from the "IRS." There is an immediate reaction from a simple word as it carries energy. It has been proven that words like *Love* and *Hate*, if written and pasted on water bottles, can alter their properties (as clinically observed in their crystalline form) from polluted to non-polluted. Similarly, words or statements such as *"I hate you"* or *"I love you"* can directly affect the properties of water, and material objects. The words coming from prayer have also been proven to be even more effective. *"In the beginning there was the Word"* reflects the deep origin of words and letters that are encoded into our DNA. These words and statements carry a unique vibration reflecting the meaning, regardless of language. Water subjected to words for twenty-four hours will clearly show a YES (Light) or NO (Dark) energy by looking at the resulting beauty (clear hexagonal shapes) or ugliness (distorted angular shapes) of the crystals. The implication here is that because we (and the planet) are 70% water, we can change the purity of water in our bodies with the simple words "Love", "Gratitude" and "Trust", the most powerful, energized words.

What has been shown to further affect this transformation process is the level of emotion attached to the words. Emotion is the common denominator to all languages, race or individuals. Emotion, or feeling, whatever it is, when created by you, is considered by Spirit to be a TRUE representation of your energy. It is the key universal communication standard understood by the Universal Mind of Spirit. A smile or a laugh is an emotional result of a human, having no difference with respect to race, religion, belief or physical state. Thus emotion generates an energy that is either an independent packet to be projected, or it can be attached to a word, thought, picture, statement or object to amplify the energy qualities. For example, associated with the energy packet are the *type, spin, polarity and intensity*. When an energy packet is created by the mind involving a word, thought, statement, object, or visualization for example, the human body becomes energy enhancer activated through the mind that adds qualities to the packet. So a word for example can have spin (negative/positive or dark/light), polarity (Yin/Yang or female/male) and intensity (strength of emotion) added to the energy packet before it is projected out to seek out its goal of finding like energy. The true mission of the Higher Self part of your mind (represented by you) or Soul is to evolve the body towards the purpose of Spirit. This, you now know is done by putting a positive spin on energy, balancing the polarity and adding genuine strong positive (love based) emotion.

We know that the focus of our awareness becomes the reality of our world. We manifest things in this world by starting with *thinking* about something, creating the *intent* to carry something out, *attracting* or seeking out the components to accomplish something and taking *action* to *manifest* it. This process is being carried out automatically through the subtle laws, or it can be accelerated by being cognizant of how to manifest or co-create proactively. The key to proactive manifestation is to use the universal language of word meaning and emotion, intensifying the energy created. That created energy, as you are about to learn, best manifests a desire when it is created by feeling the end result — what you want to manifest. In addition, the most powerful means of manifesting is to create energy packets with strong, true feelings that are without Ego, hidden motive, judgment, or desire with Ego's attachment. Because of our purpose and design, the most powerful feelings are love, compassion, forgiveness, gratitude, charity and tolerance because they are in harmony with the prime purpose and its force, adding power to the energy packet. Emotions are therefore the universal language understood by all, including Spirit.

THE LAW OF INTENT

Although emotions do not lie, combined words, and thoughts may not necessarily reflect what you are trying to communicate. Further, languages may have obscure meanings for words that distort or confuse the end meaning. This is why visualization and a feeling cannot be misunderstood. This is why it is important to add the qualities of emotional intensity to the words or thoughts. As stated under the Law of Communication, thoughts and in particular words are a communication medium to Spirit's Universal Mind — and what is referred to as the Inner World. When the thought – intent – action – manifestation sequence is initiated the crucial component that needs to be carefully considered is your *intent*. You create intent to do something and that something needs to be clear. This means that you have to pay careful attention to the energy invoked as you may inadvertently intend and manifest something that you did not really intend to. The mind in forming energy packets makes a literal translation before sending it to the Universal Mind for processing. If your thoughts or affirmations reflect a wish for more of something, then you will end up wishing. The most prevalent case in point is why more bad experiences happen when you appear to be working so hard to get rid, or resist them. Pay particular attention to the statement *"what you resist persists."* Note that this does the opposite of what you want because you are preoccupied with resistance and the energy packets are going out to attract more of the same things you are focused on. It is your focus that is wrong. The key process (as will become more apparent when you read the Law of Connection) is to state things clearly and visualize as if the goal has already been done. When you further reinforce this with positive feelings of joy experiencing this as being fact, the energy process works very diligently to *"make it so."* Believe, ask and receive. Otherwise, you bring negative manifestations of what you think you are getting rid of. Guess what *"fighting cancer"* or *"fight for peace"* or *"war on poverty"* does as a manifestation? It strengthens war and fighting by making it real. We make things happen by acknowledgement of that which we are resisting. If you focus on pain and sickness, guess what happens? Treat your mind like a big dummy, otherwise the Ego has freedom to do whatever it wants to you and your body. Create clear thoughts and instructions or pictures, and then intensify the emotional energy around them. Let me use an example. *"I feel great"* is a thought which may begin as neutral energy. If you say it with some deep breaths and begin to feel the air fill you with good feelings, you have added emotion and a positive spin to the energy. If you then stand up, stretch, breath deep, look around and feel the wonder of everything around you, you will have added strength to the feeling. And yes, science has actually measured this. Also, be aware of one more tidbit. There is one other aspect of the thoughts and words you use and the polarity applied. These are of two minds; you either give or receive. The flow direction is out or in. If a thought has both in and out, they will cancel the energy force. Example? You want to help someone but you need something (money). Make these two separate focused energies, and feel the emotion of the result. Our minds are always at work creating thoughts and energy. If you leave the mind unattended it goes to Ego autopilot. And because of the 3D world we live in where we are bombarded by negative conflictive energies, at least 85% of those thoughts will gravitate to the negative. Pay attention to this and don't let the mind in the attic get away with this. Meditation has always been the way to stop Ego interference, "going within" to truth and peace, getting in touch with the real you (Higher Self). Use it to train the Ego to balance itself with the spiritual counterpart.

THE LAW OF CHOICE

Everything you experience has a choice associated with it. Although you may not have the choice of witnessing or being part of an event (and even this can change), the interpretation or perception brought about by your experiencing any event, and the action or reaction surrounding it is a choice that is yours alone. All events are neutral. The experiences, feelings, thoughts and reactions to these events or situations create the energy packets that you assign characteristics to. How you decide to energize the packet of energy (spin, polarity and intensity) is your decision as well. More pertinent is that you can choose love based emotional energies or fear based emotional energies. With every experience you encounter, what you think, say, feel or do as a result of it, is a choice made by you. Any subsequent intent to act from that choice, and the act itself — a direct manifestation of the intent — is clearly yours. The emotions surrounding the choices come from YOUR BODY through your mind. Consider the situation where someone acts against you. Your immediate reaction is rage, aggression, or ill thoughts. Your choice of these invoke intentions to act (manifest) or follow further negative activities. However, suppose you find out the action was an attempt to protect you. All negative thoughts dissolve instantly and you would act in love, and thankfulness. The choice of interpretation, intent, action is simply yours to make and you reap what you sow. It all begins with experiencing something, creating a thought, adding the spin, adding the emotion, creating an intent to do something, then choosing the actions. By now, you will have realized that you must do everything in your power to stop negative energy from building before it attracts more — regardless of the event. You must CHOOSE to use the preferred package of emotion power words placed constantly in your mind and look for something positive that comes from it. The power words and resulting emotions should revolve around love, joy, harmony, reverence, compassion, forgiveness, gratitude and charity. These harmonize with the Laws of Purpose and reinforce good in all that happens. These, again at your choice, can be amplified even further with good feelings *coming from the heart."* They immediately dissolve negative energy AND keep you focused on accelerating the ascension track — eventually creating a snowball effect of good positive energy attracting more positive energy.

THE LAW OF REALITY

We physically live in a narrow world of what we perceive as "reality" ticking away to linear clock time within which material things appear solid. They are not. As we look deeper and deeper, we soon come to see that 95% is space — nothing. We refer to this as a 3D material world because that is what we see and touch with our senses. Our dream world, on the other hand (day or night dreams) has nothing material in it and it has no time associated with it. Close your eyes and you can visualize the dream (Inner) world. Open your eyes and you see the real (Outer) world. Your perception of these created by your mind makes your reality. Visualization is a product of the mind and it, through the mind, is the link to the Inner dream world which is the "inside spiritual world," and is also energy. The mind is a crossover between the inner "dream" world and the outer "real" world. These two worlds belong to body (real) and Spirit (dream). To the brain, which is controlled by the mind, there is no clear distinction as to whether images, visualization, dreams or what we see normally in our conscious 3D world are real or not. These are simply energy and all the same to the brain. Just as movies can make us cry, or a picture can invoke a laugh, or a dream can make us feel good, or a physical event can make us feel joy, the mind can simply invoke the brain and our physics to respond emotionally. The emotion generated in the body is real regardless of the source — and it is what is sent out to the Universal Mind for processing. The distinction of limits, time, and material quality are purely 3D limitations that we impose through our minds.

The crucial process here is to learn to visualize and emotionalize in one world, then manifest the experience we want in the other 3D world. This is why you need to be acutely aware that *"what you visualize is what you materialize."* In virtually every book or other information that discusses healing, meditation, esoterics, and even in business assertions, the process of visualization is a fundamental component of making your own reality. "Imagine" is the key operative word in making something you cannot see a reality. Now you can understand why. You are creating energy through imagining and visualization that is going to work away in the subtle Inner dream world to create what you perceive as real in your Outer material world.

What we see in the Inner dream world are all simple events or moments made of energy existing outside of linear time. Consider the analogy of a movie. A movie, or a file in a computer consists of frames or still images that are strung together to create our linear (clock) time when it is viewed. Yet the movie of two hours sitting on a file or DVD has no linear time duration associated with it until it is played. The mind cannot distinguish the difference — we do this by conscious interference and the illusion of a material construct. The choice to select your own visualizations (preferred frames or energy modules) and string them together as you wish is yours to act upon. This provides you with an ability that not only transcends time as you know it but creates boundless packets of energy visualizations reflecting opportunities, joys, and abundance that you can manifest into your own reality. The spiritual Inner world uses unrelated "moments" like our time frames in the Outer world. There are NO boundaries or limits here as there is no such thing as time. By learning to visualize and construct moment events, and experiences within this inner realm, you build the ability to manifest the imaginary into your reality — your perception of the 3D material world. Each moment or frame can further be used to generate an experience with emotion and feeling to strengthen its manifestation power of attraction. Although you can learn to constantly create this kind of "seeking" energy in your daily, conscious activities, the more ancient and traditional methods of doing this are through meditation and prayer as you are about to find out in the next law.

THE LAW OF CONNECTION

Certain words and the type of emotional energy they carry are in strict harmony with the Prime Purpose (first two laws). They carry a strong synchronization with it, making a direct connection to the Divine (Spirit). Forgiveness is such a word. When genuine strong emotion attaches itself to this word, it has tremendous power. Negative emotions stem from guilt, anger, judgment and as you now know work against the Divine Prime purposes and destroy ascension, then work towards attracting more negative energy. Anger is never justified as it is a projection of our lack of self-forgiveness. If you stop feeling guilt you stop projecting its energy. You must forgive yourself as it releases trapped energy. This release is like when you talk about something that has deep trauma. Psychologists get you on their couches to do this. Hypnosis is used the same way. The process cleanses and clears by releasing trapped negative energy that you are not aware of. So the idea is to forgive those who you believe cause a distress in you — it was an interpretation you chose anyway. Create opportunities and thoughts that reinforce your forgiveness. If you want to change something forgive the party (or you) that created the guilt, hate, anxiety, or whatever is bugging you. It is strong energy medicine. Once again be aware of your Ego that does not like this word as there is nothing to protect from, get back or be superior to. Underscore in your mind that thoughts left unattended are 85% negative so don't leave your Ego loose to generate idle thoughts that blame you or others. You are in control of the Ego (or should be) not visa versa. Stop, think, listen, choose positive. Don't *"shoot from the lip."* Don't use the *"ready, fire, aim"* mentality and be sorry later. That means you do not want to fire, then aim later! Incorporate forgiveness in your perception. There is no right or wrong, no judgment, no authority over you if you so choose. Everything we experience, we create as co-creators. To cure a disease, for example, release the emotional trauma that created it. It is the mind not the body that is sick. The body takes orders from the mind. Disease is caused by slow vibration of cells that one relates to emotional trauma, depression, and anxiety. Cancer cannot live in a high vibration, oxygen rich environment. So always forgive yourself and others. Forgiveness is thus a vital part of creating healing miracles, but it must be GENUINE. (See The Law of Miracles).

Coupled with the power of forgiveness is the powerful mode of Prayer and the Blessing. These have the direct power to alter material things and create miracles. They constitute a direct mode of communication that forms a direct connection channel to the Divine source of Spirit. It is an ancient technology that we can revitalize. First be clear that this has nothing to do with Religion. Prayer clearly is an ancient process that precedes religions – but is clearly used by them in some form. There is a reason for this. Although four common types of prayer are used by religions, the most important one – the fifth mode of "feeling" — has been deleted from the texts and knowledge bases by the rulers in power in the years around 300 AD for reasons not relevant here. It has been confirmed many times that special ancient wisdom (Tibet, Dead Sea Scrolls, Mayan, and even early Christian teachings for example) reveal this 5th mode of prayer as the most important, direct way to manifest needs. Of interest here is that prayer has four components, regardless of race, or religion. These are the *acknowledgement* (our Father in Heaven), *faith* (give us this day our daily bread), *gratitude* (Thank you for...), and a *close* (Amen) which means *"So be it"*, or *"Let it be."* In other words, what you asked for in the faith section is DONE — THANK YOU. This is why in the Law of Intent, it was important to visualize things as already done. The ancient writings by the Essenes — wisdom keepers of the Dead Sea Scrolls and original Christian belief system — made it clear that the true power of manifestation in the faith component resides in thought, emotion and feeing being *"aligned."* They said 2500 years ago: *"When thought, emotion and feeling become as one, you will say to the mountain move."* The feeling is synonymous with FAITH — something is already accomplished. Through our faith and belief, we acknowledge our power in creation — co-creators.

As an interesting reinforcement of the power of words that connect to the Divine, I offer one more tidbit of information. Ancient wisdom states that specific words in the Lords Prayer are "power words" associated with each energy center in the body (chakras). The word HEAVEN represents the upper three chakras, while the word EARTH represents the bottom three (See the Law of Balance). In the prayer itself, the words, chakras and physical body counterpart are as follows: HEAVEN, GLORY (7-pituitary), NAME, POWER (6-Pineal),

KINGDOM, WILL (5—thyroid), EVIL (4 — thymus), DEBTS (3-adrenals), TEMPTATION (2-leydig), BREAD, (1-ovaries). The energy of these words, charged with emotional energy flows through these glands to affect the psychological and physiological areas of responsibility. So when you speak directly to Spirit, every thought is treated like a prayer and every prayer is answered. There are also things happening in your body too. For example, thoughts are mental events (electrophysiological) that affect the hypothalamus causing adrenal glands to release catecholamine and activate the immune system. The electricity of thought and emotion is converted to chemicals in the brains limbic area. Thought goes to the base of the brain where a neuro transducer converts it to chemicals. A pleasant thought creates endorphins, a brain chemical 400 times more powerful than pure uncut heroin. A worried thought produces stress hormones. Science now accepts the reality of thought being bioelectrical impulses that carry information. The Universe is our physical body, and we are all cells in the body of Spirit. If all thoughts are prayers, we could say that thoughts are the electrical or energetic manifestation of each cell. Coherent thought means healthy organs/body while incongruent, or disharmonious thoughts mean dis-ease. Health occurs as disorganized thoughts become congruent. Another very interesting aspect of prayer, which is also reflected in the practice of yoga and meditation, is the position of hands. These are brought together palm to palm near the heart. What this does is to complete the subtle energy circuit between left (male) and right (female) brains so the energy balances and acts as a conduit from the heart outwards to the Universal Mind.

Another power word charged with emotion is BLESS, or the blessing. The energy of blessing is a powerful force as it sets coherence with the prime purpose, positive energy and opens the conduit to the Divine source. Much like forgiveness, the blessing frees us from the results (desires), dissolves judgment and invokes compassion. This creates powerful, highly charged love based words that accelerate ascension and act like an emotional lubricant. It becomes a point of power, moving you to a neutral position — balanced, beyond judgment, ready to talk to the Divine Intelligence. Be aware that to be truly neutral, you must bless all parties equally (victim, perpetrator, spectator) – and mean it! The process creates a special field which science now recognizes as a conduit field that carries the words directly to the source. As we move beyond a place of judgment, the words and thoughts come from a deeper place, if they carry GENUINE POSITIVE EMOTION with them! Otherwise it is a hollow statement with energy not recognized. The process of blessing makes peace with experience. It speaks directly to Spirit. Clearly, this science was known by the ancients. Teachers like Buddha and Jesus stated that: *"Compassion, gratitude, love will change your body."* It is the path to modifying your DNA which is all part of the Universal Mind. The stronger your emotion associated with the faith is, the faster things happen. The message should ring loud and clear. You need to be aware of how powerful your beliefs, thoughts and words are, for if you did, you would be more careful with these than you would be around irritated rattlesnakes. Every thought is a prayer means all thoughts are rising to Spirit. Every prayer is also answered through a collective thought process that shapes our world.

THE LAW OF MEDITATION

Meditation, like prayer has always been the way to connect with the Higher Self, neutralize the Outer World and move into the Inner World. This process is common to all cultures and brings you to a place of peace, being One with Spirit. It provides a gateway between the two worlds without sleeping, being hypnotized or being unconscious. The process of meditation lowers brain wave frequencies to exclude the noise around you and drops into a state where slow, smooth vibrations allow you to be in the space of Spirit. Here the Inner World of Spirit is boundless and timeless. This is where direct communications to Spirit becomes the purpose. You learn to link with, feel, and influence the subtle energies. This is the process referred to as "going within", or "finding the answers inside." As you reduce the frequency of brain waves and thoughts diminish, it opens silence gaps where the high frequency of Spirit, your Higher Self have a chance to enter your consciousness. Here the Higher Self which is linked to the Universal Mind and its consciousness becomes open for direct communication. In this place, there is no linear (clock) time and within it is the world of dreams, feelings, and imagination where your mind can enter a boundless realm of possibilities to experience by simply being within it. By being connected to Spirit this way you can find answers to perplexing problems. You can also work towards manifesting in your Outer World that which can be imagined in the Inner World by simply transferring it through the mind.

In old sacred texts, the ancient wisdom keepers spoke of seven sacred directions/energies that dictated the way places of worship were oriented. These had to do with harmonizing with the subtle energy forces. When meditating, position yourself according to this ancient rule. This traditional way to pray or meditate was to face east so as to activate all sides of your body's subtle energy fields. This enables you to align with and feel the Spirit forces in each direction. Energies from the east offer creative guidelines. West energies show you what you need to transform and possibly throw away. North energies will inspire you to seek challenging outcomes of the day. South energies help to support and nurture you. The fifth direction is down to the energy centre (crystal core) which gives you the unlimited powers and strength of nourishment (Mother Earth). The sixth direction is up towards the sky (The Father or Spirit) to all higher worlds and libraries in higher dimensions. The seventh is not so much a direction; it is your heart, the core centre. When you orient properly to interact with the energies and locate yourself in your heart, you can feel yourself vibrating and oscillating in tune. This entrains your body and transforms you. Your heart and mind are informed by the six sacred directions and your heart resonates with the totality of your energy field — you are fully expanded. So in the morning meditation, sit vertical facing the rising sun. Once you tune in you will be coherently attuned to the lines of force that harmonize and correct, like acupuncture fields, to derive maximum benefit of cosmic information and "tuning."

Meditation requires concentration and practice to shut out the Outer World. When you start, your brain waves will be at a Beta level of 15-35 cycles per second (cps). Here the brain is in its excited hum-drum state and blocks Spirit frequencies. As you silence and shut out the Outer World, the waves drop to the Alpha stage of 7-14 cps. Your thought forms become more powerful and contain more energy (greater amplitude). This means that any energy packets you can add to these stronger waves become more focused, intense and things become easier to manifest. The stage is typical of meditation, daydreaming, and light sleep. The next stage called Theta drops the waves to 4-7 cps which is of even slower, larger amplitude, and also very powerful but it is typical of deep hypnosis or the early portion of a sleep cycle. This stage will allow you to control body functions, is very restful and creates highly powerful creative or manifesting energy. Usually only skilled Yogis visit here. At the lowest level, called Delta, you drop to 0-4 cps reflecting deep sleep and unconsciousness. This is when one goes into a trance with no recall of their experience. In the usual practice of meditation, the objective is to get to the lower range of Alpha (7-10) where you are still conscious but in direct, most powerful communication with the Inner World and Spirit. This is where your manifestation powers are the greatest.

Meditating is a very important way to slow your life down and get to know the Genie (you). It has always been **the key way** to a peaceful and wholesome life. There are several stages of meditation which through practice will allow you to reach deeper and deeper into the Inner World. I have provided a more detailed step by step procedure with application in the section where we create a daily Mental Body Code but for the sake of being complete, I offer a summary of steps here.

Stage 1: Center yourself This means get relaxed and comfortable, align yourself with the sacred forces by facing east.

Stage 2: Be still and lower brain waves Concentrate on getting your mind chatter out of the way. Take deep breaths; take several minutes to get your body and mind slowed down.

Stage 3: Go inside the Inner World Begin your prayer or prayer equivalent by addressing Spirit, God, the Force, or whatever you want to call the Creator.

Stage 4: Bring forth your issues or needs Bring your questions and problems that require solutions into the space. If you use assertions, state these to Spirit as if they ARE done.

Stage 6: Thank Spirit, balance energy and come back out slowly Bring yourself out slowly after showing gratitude for what you have.

THE LAW OF BALANCE

There is another invisible system of subtle energy centers within the body that are sensitive to energies both inside and outside of the body. Practically all Eastern healing philosophies, and certainly the New Age healing processes recognize and attempt to balance the invisible cone shaped vortexes of energy that project backward and forward from the center vertical axis of the body. They connect our critical body organs/functions through onion-like layers of "bodies" to the universe, spirit and the life force. They are now known to perceive sensory energies and transmit impulses to nearby vital organs that control the endocrine system. They regulate many, many different body functions through the production of hormones, which are released into the bloodstream. Human psychological and physiological functions are controlled and influenced this way. They all vibrate at specific frequencies and connect with the other bodies to create a bio-electromagnetic energy system that keeps us alive and well.

Chakra	Gland	Color	Sound	Note	Essence
7 Crown	Pineal	Violet	OM or AUM	B	Spiritual Connection
6 3rd Eye	Hypo-thalamus	Indigo	MNMN	A	Intuition Awareness
5 Throat	Thyroid	Cobalt Blue	EEE	G	Commun-ication
4 Heart	Thymus	Green	AY	F	Love Expression
3 Solar Plexus	Adrenal	Yellow	AH	E	Personal Power
2 Sacral	Sexual	Orange	OOOOH	D	Sexual Capacity
1 Root	Adrenal	Red	O	C	Survival, Will to Live

A summary of their characteristics is shown in the table. Each has a specific color, musical note, vibration, sound, essence and controls specific organs in the body. The bottom three (Chakras 1 to 3) provide base functions belonging to the Outer World which your mind, in cooperation with your Ego (Lower Self) manage. The top three belong to the Inner World functions which your mind, in cooperation with Spirit (Higher Self) manage. ***The mind is the common manager and the heart is the key balance point to both.*** However, if the mind does not balance the responsibility and properly represent the non-aggressive Spirit, the Ego will take over and the higher Spirit capabilities of the top three chakras atrophy and never develop full abilities. They will also, over time, go out of balance creating psychological and physiological dysfunctions in the body.

These chakras play a vital functional role relating to physiological functions with psychological behaviors. Functioning as pumps or valves, they regulate the flow of energy through our body energy system, reflecting decisions we make concerning how we choose to respond to conditions in our life. We open and close these valves when we decide what to think, and what to feel, and through which perceptual filter we choose to experience the world around us. In terms of psychological functions, the three lower chakras are related to our raw emotions and biological instincts ranging from sexual desire and hunger, into passion, anger, pleasure and joy and other relatively simple emotional states. The four higher chakras are related to higher cognitive states. The chakras are not physical. They are aspects of consciousness in the same way that the auras are aspects of consciousness. They interact with the physical body through two major vehicles, the endocrine system and the nervous system. Each of the seven chakras is associated with one of the seven endocrine glands, and also with a group of nerves called a plexus. Thus, each chakra can be associated with particular parts of the body and particular functions within the body controlled by that plexus or that endocrine gland associated with that chakra.

All of your senses, all of your perceptions, all of your possible states of awareness, everything it is possible for you to experience can be divided into seven categories, associated with a particular chakra. Thus, the chakras represent not only particular parts of your physical body, but also particular parts of your consciousness. When you feel tension in your consciousness, you feel it in the chakra associated with that part of your consciousness experiencing the stress, and in the parts of the physical body associated with that chakra. Where you feel the stress depends upon why you feel the stress. The tension in the chakra is detected by the nerves of the plexus associated with that chakra, and transmitted to the parts of the body controlled by that plexus. When the tension continues over a period of time, or to a particular level of intensity, you create a symptom on the physical level. Now you may understand where these old heart expressions like "heartache" come from?

The chakras can become easily blocked, making you feel sick or out of balance. The **first chakra** is linked to survival instincts and our ability to ground ourselves in the physical world. Blockage manifests as paranoia, and defensiveness. The **second chakra** is related to our sexual and reproductive capacity. Blockage manifests as emotional problems or sexual guilt. The **third chakra**: gives us a sense of our personal power in the world. Blockage manifests as anger or a sense of victimization. The **fourth chakra** gives us the ability to express love. This heart chakra is related to empathy and understanding. Blockage can manifest as immune system or heart problems, or a lack of compassion. The **fifth chakra** is directly tied to creativity and communication. It is related to vocal expression, hearing, and the ability to communicate. Blockage manifests as problems like laryngitis or sore throats, creative blocks or general problems communicating with others. The **sixth chakra** is the seat of intuition and awareness. It is related to discriminative cognition and the ability to understand. Blockage manifests as sinus or eye problems. The **seventh chakra** is related to one's personal spiritual connection to the universe. It is also related to understanding and comprehension, but as well serves as an integrative factor. This is a rough outline but I think you get the point. If you have symptoms like these, you can rebalance chakras through meditation and paying strict attention to creating positive energies.

You may have noted the heart chakra is situated between the Higher (Spirit) and Lower (Ego) functions. Ancient lore said the heart is considered the source of emotion, courage and wisdom. It is the core of the body and has a subtle energy system. It is therefore the balancing point, as noted in the 7 Sacred Directions. Science has now confirmed the heart and nervous systems DO NOT follow the brain's direction. The Heart has its own brain that communicates with and influences the cranial brain. The heart's electromagnetic field is 60 times greater in amplitude than the electrical activity of the brain. The magnetic field produced is 5000 times greater in strength than the field generated by the brain. The field centered on the heart chakra is an independent torus of energy that can reach 6-8 feet in radius and possibly miles in terms of subtle energies. The heart can sense, remember, learn, feel, receive and process information independently. It is the most powerful generator of rhythmic information patterns in the body. The heart communicates four ways through the neurological (nerves), biophysical (pulse wave), biochemical (hormones) and energetic (electromagnetic) systems in the body. It uses the ANS (Autonomic Nervous System) to affect the digestive, cardiovascular, immune and hormonal systems. Thoughts and subtle emotions influence balance and activity of ANS. Negative emotions create disorder in the autonomic nervous system that affect the rest of the body creating disharmony, inefficiency and increased stress. Positive emotions create increased balance and efficient brain function creating harmony and coherence in rhythms, where increased coherence creates shifts in perception and ability to deal with stress (mental clarity, creativity, balance, effectiveness). The degree of coherence measured through the heart rate variability (HRV) between mind and emotion is critical. Unmanaged emotional stress such as anger and anxiety have been shown to be six times more predictive of cancer and heart disease than other killers like smoking or hypertension. These emotional problems impede information flow. So your emotional system can be developed into coherence by controlling emotion. By now you know this clearly; the most powerful emotions are love, compassion, and forgiveness. Self generating positive emotions generate coherence. *"I love you from the bottom of my heart"* is one of the most powerful energy focused feelings on the planet.

There is ancient technology behind such statements and many other expressions involving the heart. You now know why. There is a physiological reaction from the heart center that you feel physically. The process of "entrainment" is well known in science. If you had a roomful of clocks with pendulums, at the start they would all swing out of synchronization. If you came in the next day, they would all be swinging together. That is called entrainment. A new sub-frequency amplifying and harmonizing the other synchronized frequencies is created out of nowhere. When you entrain your body, mind and spirit by getting the love and compassion energy in your heart on the same wave length, multiple chemical, biological, physcological and spiritual frequencies entrain creating a symphony of coherent oscillating systems. Heart-head entrainment is brought about by appreciation and love. The Alpha brain waves are synchronized to the cardiac cycle. It has been proven that when people touch (or in proximity) one person's heart beat signal is registered in the other's brainwaves. When the coherence is good, intuitive listening is enhanced. When coherence is poor (anger, stress hatred, anxiety) the result is incoherent signals thereby affecting the physical responsibilities of the heart chakra. What does this mean? Obesity, diabetes, hypertension, digestive disorders, and arterial dysfunction are some starters. Care and compassion boosts immune system, reduces cortisol. This is also why classical music harmonizes – it influences the heart's subtle system as it affects emotion and mood states. Studies have shown that rock music does the opposite – generating anger and conflict.

THE LAW OF EGO

The Ego you now know is commonly referred to as the Lower Self. It is your co-manager in the Outer World while the Higher Self (connected directly to Spirit) is your co-manager of the Inner World. The Ego is an invisible mental construct, a part of the mind that deals with your survival in the physical world. It has instinctual automatic abilities to control body functions. This Ego is one of three parts and functions as a counterpart to the mind that YOU are supposed to control. The Ego, by design, has a primary purpose of protecting you from threats and insuring that you manifest a safe existence by directing the bottom three chakras of survival, reproduction, and power. Its task is to find a balance between its two counterparts, the super-Ego and the id. While the Super-Ego acts as the conscience, maintaining our sense of morality and the prohibition of taboos, the

Id is the source of our drives considered to be the reservoir of libido — predominantly sexual that underlies all mental processes (so said Freud).

Over time, and due to the stress ridden world we live in, we have let the Ego loose to create what is called Duality — a separation of us from the spiritual world, thus clearly severing the body from the Soul or Higher Self. The Ego has accentuated this duality by bringing thoughts about competition, protection, betterment and other survival mechanisms that create an urgent desire for material possessions first and foremost in your mind. This falls strongly to the "dark side" and overrides the upper chakras, limiting the growth on the spiritual side and losing a proper balance between upper and lower chakras. It is for that reason that regardless of good or bad energy, as a goal, competition, protection, survival, and morals have evolved with little regards to the light side and the Ego has effectively dominated the evolutionary plan. The heart chakra and energy center are the balance point which are essentially ignored, as are suggestions from the Spirit side. To bring the situation back into balance, the heart needs to filter the Ego's dominant thoughts. And if you are to follow the Universal Laws of Love and Ascension, the Ego must not be allowed to manage and direct all the functions of the powerful energy generators that not only manifest wrong things for you but can end up creating dysfunction and disease in the body.

Let me explain this in another way. The issue is that for whatever reason, you being in charge of the mind, have not managed the show by properly balancing the work load. The division of responsibilities is off-whack. The advice from your Higher Self (Spirit) to develop the spirit side is not balanced with the advice from the Ego to develop the material 3D side. Spirit is represented by the Soul or Higher Self, which resides in the Inner World. It is not aggressive like its counterpart, the Lower Self or Ego that dominate the physical Outer World. Remember, the Higher Self represents Spirit and it is strictly a love based phenomenon. It will not demand, conflict, judge, or fight. So the Ego's thoughts are always fired out first and the Higher Self can only try to correct or suggest another option which will come out later — if you give it a chance! What has most likely happened is that the Ego, being dominant, has taken over YOUR management function, overrides the Spiritual functions and conducts the whole orchestra on your behalf. It is simply doing what it feels is best for it and does with the body whatever it sees fit to accomplish its task. You may now understand a bit better what is meant by my expression: *"You are fired said the Heart to the Ego, you have been measured, you have been weighed and judged and you have been found wanting."* The Ego has become too overzealous with its importance. Your body — and your true abilities as well as your organs it controls — have suffered as a result.

The requirement here is to take your responsibility back and balance the Inner with the Outer worlds by using the heart as your key consultant. Take control of the orchestra, play the right classical music and balance the functions between Ego and Spirit. Then your body can begin to recover. The Higher Self needs you to impose the rules. If you do not show the intent to choose this, then the Ego will simply take over and dominate the three major energy centers of the heart, brain and chakras. And by now, you must realize that this is not necessarily in your best interest, and certainly not in the best interest of the Higher Self.

THE LAW OF MIRACLES

Forgiveness and prayer are reported to be key ingredients to facilitating healing miracles. This as you have understood from the Law of Connection, is because you are opening up a direct channel to Spirit — the Divine source. The most amazing miracles have been documented to be Divine based with no explanation and occur almost "instantly." In looking at miracles themselves, they are common in every race, religion and culture. Just about everyone has heard of a miraculous story where someone has been healed in some unexplainable fashion. The Indian cultures of South America report these. The Religions of the East and West report these. The Native American Indigenous people report them. The tribes of Africa report these, as do people in China, Tibet, and India. The list is endless and it bridges all races. Now even science and hospitals report these. Near death experiences report these. What is the common element? It is forgiveness, compassion, faith and a connection with God, the "force" or Great Spirit made through ceremony, meditation, prayer, rituals, or some mode of Divine communication. How does it occur? A highly compelling course called a *Course on Miracles* says it is virtually impossible for our narrow 3D minds to understand, let alone believe how this happens. It states that at one instant in time, two major scripts were written like a movie. One movie was based on the destructive Ego mind of the material world and the other was based on a clean version by the Spirit mind. So for everything done by Ego, there is a corrected, clean version compiled by Spirit. Everything in the past and the future has already happened. Admittedly, that is a tough concept to accept! It goes on to state that what has not yet happened is which parts of the movie we are going to choose and how we experience it. The link to the Spirit side is through FORGIVNESS. How do you suddenly "pick" a miracle from the clean, non-diseased script? Get good at forgiveness, love, compassion and working towards the higher good on the Spirit script. It is the strength of that love and forgiveness, with conviction of love based actions and the emotions surrounding them that give you the power to flip.

Science speculates that time as we know it — we call it linear time — is only real because of the way we perceive it. We follow clocks as it is how things work in our 3rd Dimension. Think about this as a DVD sitting on a pile. One of those DVDS is made up of a movie, which is made up of millions of frames (pictures) that when strung together and played, give you a movie of two hours taking up linear time. While the DVD sits there it has no time associated with it. It simply exists. Now the creator of this DVD could have also strung these frames together in a different sequence to make a different movie. As we become lighter (higher vibrations, ascend, create more "space" between electrons) we eventually get to the 4th Dimension which is where there is no time as we perceive it. Science suggests that time (going forward and backward) has a third vertical component that we are not able to tap into yet. This means that at each moment, there are an infinite number of possibilities. However, let us go back to the DVD stack and say there are many DVDs stacked here that we can choose from and that on each DVD there are different frames that can be chosen at any moment. As we move from moment to moment in our daily lives, we are selecting the frames off a DVD. But what if we can just select or jump to any one of these frames or sequences by choice. The suggestion here is that there already exists all the possibilities (as we are choosing now) but there are others such as those that occur when miracles take place. In other words, there is an alternative available that you can jump to. So if you have a diseased organ for example, there exists a parallel frame set where it is not diseased. A case in point is an example of healing practices in Japan. Three practitioners in a hospital planned to get rid of a three inch cancer ulcer in the bladder of a woman. Ultra sound images showed results while a monitor was injected to show progress. The three practitioners and the woman entered a state of focused meditation visualizing a clear bladder and uttered a phrase "already done." The tumor quivered and disappeared in under three minutes. They succeeded in flipping to a new set of frames.

There is yet another "mind bending" thought I leave you with. The work done by Gregg Braden on the Torah, the first five books of the Hebrew bible — part of the Dead Sea Scrolls, is relevant and profound. It is suggested that all that was and all that will be is in the Torah. The work uses computers and ELS (Equidistant Letter Sequences) to extract one letter a fixed number of letters apart from one long string of characters (300,000 letters) representing the Torah – without regards to space or punctuation. The extracted results create "squashed" sentences which have predicted specific events, names and timings with an amazing, unbelievable accuracy. How do we "time jump" to a miracle frame? Ask with TRUE forgiveness in your heart and you shall receive. At the end of this booklet we will revisit this topic.

YOUR NEW LIFE CODE

Now you know why the book has a subtitle of *"Talking Heart to Heart."* It has the largest and strongest field and the *"emotion of the heart"* is highly potent energy, synchronized with the laws of love and ascension. You can now understand why the heart and its positive emotion is such an important component of all of this. It should be clear that it IS the REAL ENERGY FORCE that needs to be managed within the laws it was set up to abide by. Anything else simply has repercussions to your mind, body, spirit AND your resultant life — your quality time! It should also be clear that to ignore it is folly. Your journey to continuous quality time is through this door. It appears simple but the continuous discipline required to walk this talk is not simple. You must reprogram your mind and body. But remember this clearly: Deploying a new Life Code through a simple, carefully laid out plan is your Genie in the bottle and it is available to you at any time. It is simply a matter of choice. And when you start rubbing the magic lamp, this Genie has endless wishes to manifest at your command, not just three. You, my dear reader, ARE the Genie.

Now, there are many more Laws and energy centers but what I have laid out here is your starting point. And if you launch a program that integrates these laws into your daily routine, you will begin to discover a new life unfolding around you. But now the big question is HOW? How does one set up the CODE — a simple program routine to comply with all the laws and entrain the body, mind and soul into creating more quality time AND manifesting desired experiences? Does one have to pray or meditate on a mountain top all day like a monk? NO! Let me tell you something about enlightened people. They are WHOLE and unimposing. They simply KNOW who they are. They are totally present in the moment, radiating joy and compassion without judgment. They have highly developed cosmic wisdom and have a direct contact with the Divine. They have freedom from inner conflict, are liberated from the past, and have no sensitive points that trigger Ego based emotions. They are keen on promoting happiness and enlightenment. They are not engaged in the tension, conflict and aggression that materialism brings. You will FEEL their presence in your heart center.

So back to the question of HOW? The next sections set up a simple, complete Life Code as a daily routine that you can modify for yourself. My suggestion is to do this later, after you have used it for a while and understand the discipline required. It is designed to integrate all of the laws into a daily routine for you. As you read this part, you will begin to see the correlation with the laws. You should begin to see how, if you pay attention to your thoughts, emotions and motivations, things around you will begin to change. You will begin to see the real power in these simple laws and practices.

By now you may have realized that the Subtle Laws of the Universe in conjunction with your Ego have been conductors playing their own symphonies. They have been playing your life tunes (drama) more than you realized. They were designed to work in harmony and play a grand symphony but you have more than likely relinquished your control. And the Ego has undoubtedly had a lot to do with the conducting — at the expense of its audience (your cellular structure). So, you say, how can one possibly make a plan that works with all of these complicated laws? Well, if anything should read loud and clear by now, it is the role of your MIND and EMOTION that is the serious consideration. You simply have to break some old habits on what you say, think and believe, AND how you generate emotions. We have unfortunately made this difficult for these laws to operate as they were designed to do. And by now you will have realized that what you have achieved in your life is a result of your habits and thoughts — and your beliefs. It may also be apparent that this process may have been more influential in determining what you are than you figured before. For some, you may have realized that your "think and grow rich", "business assertions", and "taking control of your life" courses deploy some of these laws. For others perhaps on the religious side, you will have realized that some of this, particularly the prayer and blessing side may not be new as well. But much more important is that if you want quality time, these transcend every difference on the planet. You must be very aware not to move to the "dark side." You do not want to give the most powerful energy generators around — your mind/brain and your heart — negative energy of ANY kind to work on!

The CODE involves three main areas of better well-being. This **"trinity of well-being"** leads to everything else. They are **SPIRIT, BODY and MIND.** They are most likely not synchronized together. They need to work in harmony with you and your beliefs. Now, like any plan, there has to be some thinking ahead of time so as to execute a proper implementation of the CODE. Let me present the three segments of the Trinity separately and how to build your "operating code" that will reprogram your bio-computer AND put you into proper position as Conductor of the symphony. I want you to understand that the Code I present has absolutely nothing to do with religion, any particular culture, discipline or science. This Code is about a common wisdom reflected in all sources. It is my attempt to rationalize the common denominators into a plan of daily action that will respect all the laws.

THE SPIRIT CODE

There are some important components of creating an effective spiritual healing and nourishment plan that require a bit of up-front thinking. The first major component of the complete plan is to think about growing and nourishing the Spirit. It already has a strong purpose and base of existence reflected in the first two laws of **Purpose**, which are Ascension and Love. The other laws are laws of **Process** — the way things work. In setting up your overall Spiritual plan, there are some key components.

Component One: Define your underlying belief system

How are you going to synchronize your life with the first Subtle Laws of Ascension and Love? What do you stand for? What do you feel is important to your life in going forward? It is important to set an overall scene of coherence to your belief system. In other words *"walk the talk."* If you are going to preach love, then you need to believe what you preach otherwise it is all a façade and it will create discord, and disharmony as there are certain parts to you that cannot be fooled. Remember, discord and incoherence create dis-ease. You can't preach peace and engage in fighting. So what do you believe in? Is it the Ten Commandments? What makes up your morals, code of ethics, basic beliefs, your truths? These are up to you but do they include a philosophy of respecting other's life, liberty and property? Do they include respecting other's pursuit of happiness, and living your life in such a way as to always do unto others as you would expect them to do unto you? Do they project love and service? What I am saying here is that you do not want to pay lip service to your belief system. If you are part of the Divine creation then believe and act that way. If you are here to learn your way to your Divinity, then believe it. If love and peace are your fundamentals, then believe it and live it. What I am trying to convey here is that manifesting a better life and creating more quality time goes a lot smoother and faster if you start with a belief system that becomes YOUR commandments. And the best way to optimize your progression to a quality life is to be in harmony with the Laws of Purpose. You need an underlying mission and a grander purpose. I cannot dictate this as every culture, race, and religion has a different value system. BUT when you lay this out, think in terms of Life, Liberty, Property and the pursuit of happiness as YOUR right and everybody else's. If you make it simple and integrate peace, love and forgiveness into this belief, the rest is just noise.

Component Two: Place the Ego in its proper place
You now understand what is meant by my expression: *"You are fired said the Heart to the Ego, you have been measured, you have been judged, weighed and you have been found wanting."* The Ego has specific duties and responsibilities and must report to YOU. You represent the Spiritual side and the heart is your consultant. Imbed this as your Code and keep this truth foremost in your mind at all times. Love and Ascension are the rule. The Ego must not be allowed to manage and direct the functions of the powerful energy generators that not only manifest things for you but can end up creating dysfunction and disease in the body. As to discriminating which is which, the Ego is always first up, Spirit second. Spirit's is ALWAYS a good thought. This is a philosophy that you must WRITE deep into your CODE.

Component Three: Synchronize your beliefs and habits with the positive part of the Subtle energy control centers
If you recall the Law of Balance you will remember what the Chakra energy centers have responsibilities for. These must be healed to be spinning open and balanced to function properly. The process of doing this is included as part of the MIND CODE which will follow. But most important, once they are functioning properly, a CODE of

behavior needs to be made that ensures balance between the Male (Yang) and Female (Yin) energies are maintained and have a POSITIVE spin. This needs to become a strong philosophy where your awareness is simply "on guard for negative intruders."

Component Four: Develop the experiences you want that will give you more Quality Time

So now we come to what you want out of life, and hopefully things that are going to nurture the Spirit. Lay out what you desire out of life. Do you want more money? Do you want more love? It is up to you. Remember, there is no judgment on what you do or want. It is your choice, BUT if you move to the positive light side of life, you will find that things happen easier and they will be more meaningful. This is very important. You need to sit down and write out what it is you want in your life. No one can do this but you. Decide what your ideal body, attitude and health would be. Decide what your day, should look like. Decide what an ideal mental attitude would be. Consider disposition, thinking, and so on. Decide your spiritual ideal. **Decide what you want to experience.**

Now I have to help you a bit here in that being true to *your* heart is the formula for living the life you want. When there is an alignment between what is in your heart and the actions you carry out, the better life will work. You're fulfilled, content and at peace. You feel care, appreciation, love, joy, compassion, kindness — heart-felt emotions that not only feel good, but are also good for you too. So as you go through your list, start by considering what you value most and are they synchronized with those core values.

Think about this as a Universal Catalogue of Experiences and make your order list. It could be ascension, health, being a healer, spiritual avatar, car, house, job, money, love, business, success, writing a book... whatever. These are things you feel will provide you with an experience that gives you quality time. When you have identified one, there are three important things needed.

First, you must IDENTIFY it. Be clear about what it is; the best way is to write it down very clearly in a concise statement. For example you may want to have a new car, perhaps a new Corvette. Second, you need to have a clear PICTURE of the END RESULT of having attained it. In this case the visual representation could be a picture or image of a new red Corvette. The third part is to bring in the emotional part. Visualize a clear picture of you sitting in or driving your Corvette and **FEEL** the great experience of it – the wind in your face, feeling the great outdoors. What you must capture are the feelings that you would have as a result of having it. So once this is done, these items reflect what components of your life are to provide you with the experiences of quality time you desire. Once you have your initial list, these can be combined into an imaginative sequence where you can create a thought, visualization, emotion and feeling for each. This is how you make a little **Quality Time Movie** if you like. It may be a good idea to write a little script of this movie and read it to make sure it is what you want. You will need this for the Mind Code that follows.

THE BODY CODE

Know that your body is the Sacred Temple. Learn to treat it like you would any other precious Temple. You have been given this miraculous physical machine that is not by any means operating close to its full potential. And no matter who you are, or what shape you are in, this statement is true. With the exception of miracles, there is no magic pill to immediately fix what you have so diligently spent many years trying to impede. If your body is anything like anybody else's, it has been abused, contaminated, and stressed for many years. So fixing this is going to require some effort. I am sure you have heard this before but you need to de-contaminate, tune it and maintain it properly. Here are your key components:

Component One: Love your body
It is your temple and it is unique. Remember, it responds best to love and peace. It has capabilities and abilities that you are not aware of so treat it as a very precious thing. Remember also that you have to love yourself and your body first before anybody else loves it. Understand that the way you **feel about** it is directly affecting or infecting its incredible capabilities. It is your choice. Understand clearly that you do not have any idea of its real capabilities. Know this because it is true and it is only your limited scope of understanding that prevents it from attaining its true capabilities. Feel good about it. A highly effective way of doing this is to take 30 seconds per day, close your eyes, join your palms in front of your heart and state (or think) using your own name: *"Ed, I love you, Ed, I thank you, Ed, I respect you"* several times and feel the 70% water in your body cleanse.

Component Two: Decontaminate your body
You have spent most of your life contaminating it with bad fuel and stress. You may want to go to a naturopath or dietician and find out what your food sensitivities are.

If you are overweight or unhealthy, you will probably find that the stuff you like best is the worst for you. That is your Ego running the show. Don't feed that little monster first. Get your body to tell you how it feels, not your Ego. What's the difference? The first beer tastes really good. The fourth beer is the Ego telling you that you need one more for the road while your body is saying Oh No! The body may thank you for a new eating plan and it all goes to giving the body a chance to get into a better state so it can perform what it was designed to perform. It was designed to heal itself but if your machinery is not functioning well because of a lack of proper physical and spiritual food, it becomes dysfunctional, lowers its vibration and becomes susceptible to dis-ease. Look for ways of cleansing, and detoxifying as a "kick-start" plan to get it to the point where it is capable of doing its job. Booze, drugs, processed foods, high acidity foods, smoking are well-known contaminators and polluters. Make a plan to moderate them.

Component Three: Exercise your body
The muscles, and particularly the main "pump" or heart simply need exercise to function well. If that engine is not attended to then you know the result. Even if it is a walk in the park 2-3 times a week, the body will thank you for it. Your body is designed to perform as an incredible machine, but it needs to be worked to work well. It will quickly atrophy its functionality if you don't. You can certainly choose your own plan as to what you do but make it a habit, like a ritual. It has to be a physical activity and it works hand in hand with number 5 below.

Component Four: Water your body
A regular amount of water helps to flush the junk out of the body and the organs have less of a tendency to get overloaded preventing toxins from accumulating. A high majority of people do not take in anywhere near enough to help flush so of course, many little bad guys like

heavy metals and toxins like to build up a strong team to inhibit function. Eight glasses a day is an average. Your organs will thank you as this is the way they avoid overload and dysfunction. A rule of thumb is to take your weight in pounds, divide it in half to yield the number of ounces per day of water needed. Simply make this a habit.

Component Five: Ventilate your body

The blood needs oxygen to work well and feed the rest of the system. If it does not receive sufficient oxygen, it cannot transfer air and food into the rest of the system and itself becomes dysfunctional. Deep pranic breathing and aerobic activity helps get more of this fuel into the blood so it can do what it was designed to do, namely make the body work. You may not know this but the real transfer of spiritual essence and deep energy takes place when you hold your breath for 3-4 seconds AFTER you take your breath (deep pranic breathing). Just think how many breaths you have wasted! If the blood cannot transfer oxygen, digest things properly, get rid of unwanted foreign contaminants, it goes into a stress condition that begins to create dysfunction in the major organs that it is supposed to serve. You can't fire old "Pumpy" for not performing so things usually get worse until they break. To give Pumpy power, help him. From best to good is skipping, running, bikes, aerobics, or walking. Take your choice of cure but DO IT. Your blood will thank you for it. You will digest food better and get more oxygen. Even when you are stressed, deep breathing will calm you.

Component Six: Nourish your body with proper food

This is where you need to start thinking seriously about that hard fuel that the body needs. The Ego likes to conduct the orchestra here but you know it would set up a diet of chocolate bars, ice cream and fries for you if you let it. Most don't let it get away with this kind of tune but it always likes to try another "craving" on you.

Don't listen. Your body may have been vibrating to the Ego's tune too long and it cannot even tell you what it needs. A Dietician or Naturopath can tell what is best for your body type and what is not. Get on the natural, the organic, and the wholesome stuff. As mentioned earlier, you may have some pretty bad habits that are silently working away to slow your machinery down to the point where something breaks. The statement *"you are what you eat"* is highly appropriate. Eat junk food and you will rapidly prepare your body for the junk pile. The food you give it is all it can use to work with, so if you believe it is your temple, treat it so with the right fuel it needs to look and feel like the temple it is. You do not have to go on crash diets and extreme plans. You need to make a moderate, dedicated food plan and stick with it. A friend once said: *"When it comes to push and shove, the best diet is to push and shove less food in your mouth."*

Component Seven: Calm your body
We know stress does not help the body. As you now understand, stress, anxiety, worry, and fear are the worst trouble makers around as they lower vibrations and set the stage for the other bad guys – diseases – to get established. The most important activities to engage in to calm it are **Meditation** and **Mother Nature**. I will cover meditation later. Get out and be One with Mother Nature. Don't get old, get outdoors! The key word here is REVERENCE. Use your senses to see it, feel it, smell it, hear it and wonder at it. Nature is one of the greatest dividend payers on the planet. Go out and learn to hug a tree. Make it a habit to get into Nature and merge with it... and leave your cell phone behind! Make a ritual of this little sanctuary with Nature. Really feel it and understand the grand beauty of it all. Get a dog! Dogs are trained stress reducers and nature lovers.

As a summary, it is not my intention here to provide a specific dietary and physical program. What is more important is that **YOU** take the responsibility into **YOUR** hands and design **YOUR OWN PHYSICAL BODY** program that follows the components above. Everybody is different, at a different stage of health and has their own needs. BUT, the bottom line is that you need to make a consistent effort to think about your body code, lay it out and MANIFEST it. It should be easy because it is entirely up to YOU.

THE MIND CODE

Coupled with the Spirit and body is your mind. The plan has to work both components together. Remember you are what you think and your mind is the real Conductor of your reality. When you pollute and encumber these bodies with negative energy, they manifest in poor heath, bad attitude, disharmony... you know the result. When they are in harmony, working together, they are extremely powerful in manifesting things beyond your normal belief. Here are the key components.

Component One: Unplug from the Matrix
The Matrix is all around you in your daily life making you react with anger, hate, anxiety, and fear. The Matrix feeds you information that makes you judge, take sides, feel inadequate, compare and always look for more. This is the Ego's influence as it can never be satisfied. The Matrix is designed to get you to consume more and generate doubts about your accomplishments. That constant deluge is how the mind has been trained to generate 85% negative thoughts if you let it alone. Look for ways to unplug — change the channel — from this constant bombardment. Learn to think before you react and convert any negative energy to positive energy. Resist negative influence and an incessant drive towards conflict and stress. It will serve you better. It is simply your choice. The media drives your emotions through TV, movies, radio, and newspapers. Bad news, violent shows, crime, and other distressing mind junk feed you a steady diet of negative energy that you assimilate into your mind and body like a sponge. Two serious things are happening here. Your thoughts are attracting like energy as do negative emotions and these are generating disharmony in your body preventing you from reaching higher abilities. Unplug yourself from this. Make a conscious effort to change the channel. You do not need negative emotions. This generates more hatred, conflict, fear and negative manifestations that you are

not aware of. Rather than be a TV couch potato where your body and Ego get junk food, pick programs that give you warm toasty feelings, goose bumps, tingles and a buzz. Wean yourself.

Component Two: Monitor your feelings
If something is good, it will generate good feelings. Your emotional and physical bodies are a good judge. If something does not feel good and you cannot make it so, delete it, reflect it back and do not succumb to it. You know there are two opposite energy force groups. One is **LOVE energies** of *love, reverence, gratitude, charity, joy, forgiveness, and harmony*. They build and reinforce positive energy. These put a positive spin on energy which raises vibrations. The opposite is the **FEAR** energies of *fear, hate, greed, anger, despair, and anxiety*. These are unwanted energies that you must consciously banish. Always be aware of negative energies and when you feel them, STOP, THINK and CHOOSE a way of nullifying them before they get you going in the wrong direction, and take their orders to seek out more of the same. Whenever you are about to react in a negative fashion and create an emotion, or speak, **pause a few seconds** and recall the notion that *"energy flows where attention goes."* Take a few deep breaths and watch the thoughts. Unless you are a masochist for grief, this should stop you instantly. Then process the thought and emotion through the heart before it becomes an unruly generator of negative manifestations. Train the brain and choose a positive spin in life. If you have a very serious problem, leave it alone for 2-3 days, then come back to it for a new look. Also see the following practice of resolving problems and issues below.

Component Three: Make the Ego report to the Heart
This aspect requires repeating because of its importance. Become the watcher of reactive thought energy. Clearly, if your life is balanced to the negative side (fear, anger, conflict, hate, anxiety, etc.) manifesting in health issues, lack of quality time, the Ego has not served you well.

Obviously, it has not served the Spiritual side well either. The message here is that Ego needs to be reporting to the heart. What does this mean? Whenever you have any thoughts or reactions that upset you, STOP and filter it through the heart center first. Before the trigger of intent releases the energy AND actions (or reactions) check with the heart to see if you can convert it to a positive energy/action. YOU control the Ego. So take control of it and monitor it because unless you take the role of control, it will simply do its thing, release the negative energy, amplify it with emotion, trigger the intent, send it out to seek out more, and manage the body functions accordingly.

Component Four: Take your time of Personal Peace
In following up on the last item under Physical, you need to start training your mind to slow down and pay attention to a new environment. Meditation, coupled with prayer is a powerful process and is your primary grounding with healing the mind and body. *I want to underscore that this is NOT a religious process or tied to any particular race or culture. It is a PROCDURAL PROCESS that you can call anything you like.* Although I am referring to it as meditating, it is your Peaceful Time where you make your transition to the Inner World. Do it regularly and faithfully. To get your mind in the right frame, my suggestion is that you should allocate two 30 minute blocks of time. One in the morning sitting facing east. and one in the evening, lying down, before you go to sleep. What is important is that this time becomes a habit, like another regular little ritual. Meditating is very important and it has been **the key way** to a peaceful and wholesome life. It is the way to get in touch with your Higher Self, go inside, and become One with Spirit. The process lowers your brain waves into a mode of relaxation where daily life is effectively blocked out. This is when you learn to get in touch with the real you and enter the Inner World of spirit and boundless possibilities. Every day when you find your place of peace to meditate quietly, sit and visit your Temple. You

will become better and better at visiting the peace inside. Know this is where you initiate your manifestations by simply believing, asking, feeling the joy of being and receiving. You can eventually, say after a month, design your own meditation scheme but I have tried to simplify a starting program for you to follow in the morning before breakfast. It is YOUR PERSONAL PEACEFULL TIME. Follow the guidelines below:

Stage 1: Center yourself This means get relaxed and comfortable. Put on some soft music, get quiet and into a space where you are disconnected from external noises and distraction. To align yourself in harmony with subtle forces and the sacred directions, face East. This is like entrainment to maximize and make coherent the energy fields. If you want to place your palms together near your heart to facilitate the connection as in Yoga, do so here.

Stage 2: Be still and lower brain waves Here you concentrate on getting your mind buzz and thought fuzz out of the way. You can concentrate on your breathing or repeat something (mantra) like a key word or phrase to focus on getting rid of the outside, especially the noise the Ego has to contribute. Take 3 deep breaths into the chest and lower area through the nose, hold it for 4-5 seconds and breathe out through your mouth. This will give the life energy time to transfer into you. This may take several minutes but you need to get your body and mind slowed down into the Alpha wave range. If you need to visualize a nice beach or something to help focus on getting still, that's fine.

Stage 3: Go inside the Inner Realm Begin your prayer or prayer equivalent by addressing Spirit, God, the Force, or whatever you want to call the Creator. This is where you can start using key power words to change the properties of your water (70%

of you) by stating your name with "*I love, you, I thank you, I respect you.*" Let Spirit know you are there, entering the Temple and that you are One with it. This is where you have lowered your brain waves and are now in the proper frame of mind and body to speak and feel in the inner realm. Be patient, it takes practice to slow down and feel the silence. Relax and feel the simple silence. Activate your heart center and feel it expand to radiate love and peace to the planet. State that you love yourself as you do Spirit as you are One. Bless ALL the people on the planet and forgive everyone for their angers, conflicts and hostilities.

At this point, you can set a routine that deals with the chakra energy centers. To function in an optimum manner, these need to be opened fully, spinning strongly and balanced. So, your visualization routine here is to start at the bottom (root chakra) breathe in the energy of the Universe to the base and accumulate it. Then make a connection to the core of the earth, into that base energy. After several breaths, and an accumulated pool of energy, visualize the light energy moving upwards, through the next higher chakra progressively as you exhale. Go from root, sacral, solar plexus, heart, throat, brow areas to the top of the head. Each time you visualize, think and feel the energy vortex of the chakra opening, spinning and balancing as each breath is exhaled. Try to feel the energy rising and circling. Each breath draws new energy into the pool, moving to a higher chakra as you push and clean upwards. At the end of this sequence, you will still be connected to the earth for nourishment (Mother energy), you will project your energy through the top crown chakra into the source (Father energy) and be properly balanced.

You now know that the Inner Spiritual World has no boundaries and is not limited by linear time, science, beliefs, or anything we are used to. This presents a secret place where you can deploy your imagination as you wish and get better and better at "going inside" where Spirit and your soul reside. This is where you get better and better at lowering your brain waves to lower and lower points, activating higher and higher functions. This is where you go to Alpha waves or lower. When you learn to enter properly, you will effectively be able to talk to the Universal Intelligence and your DNA.

Stage 4: Bring in your issues and manifestation plan Here is where you can clearly identify your problems and issues, asking for solutions. Ask, pause and listen. The answer may come then or later through events, people, and ideas. If you use assertions, state these to Spirit as if they ARE done. Examples are: I AM healed. I HAVE prosperity. I FEEL healthy, I AM happy. I ATTRACT goodness. This is when you visualize your life movie in as many frames as you can create that reflect completion. As you play your movie, visualize the end results, strengthen the power of manifestation by feeling the positive emotions of the result completed. Activate the heart center by the emotion — make it stronger and stronger. You get better at as you concentrate. Remember that this inward process can become more and more effective so that you can even ask and receive in your normal activities outside of meditation. Enjoy your movie. Be patient and relaxed. Keep your focus and attention. The mind will begin to attract the energy of events, answers, opportunities and people that will lead to a manifestation of your needs. If you have a specific meditative program, here is where you place it. You get better at it as you concentrate.

Stage 5: Thank Spirit, balance energy, and come back out slowly When you are ready to get back into the outside world, after 20-30 minutes, bring yourself out slowly. Before you come out, show gratitude for what you have. Thank Spirit for the answers to your assertions, problem solutions and life movie. You are showing gratitude for having your solutions and your movie DONE. You are showing gratitude for what you already have. Then, starting from the floor where you are grounded, allow your awareness and your energy to slowly float upward through your body core all the way up to the crown of your head. Feel the energy perfectly balanced. You are at peace and you can now expand to full awareness of the Outer world around you.

Component Five: Build a positive spin philosophy into your life

The manifestation of your needs reduce down to a simple life code. You must constantly be on guard to monitor your feelings to make sure the vibratory engines are being fed a steady diet of love and positive emotions. When any event or situation occurs that creates fear, anger, greed, hostility or the likes, immediately stop your thought and reaction process and look to something good that comes of it. Build resilience against the FEAR energies. Keep your heart center filled with strong emotions of love, compassion, gratitude and joy. To support your life plan outside of meditation, gather any kind of visual material that reinforces the end result of your wishes. For example if it is a new home you want or 1 million a year in income, or health, place a representative picture of it in front of you during your work (or play) day. Dream the end results, visualize them, see them, smell them, feel them, touch them... use your daily 5-sensory system as if they were real. Keep the heart center radiating for miles. Then let the natural law of energy attraction bring the events to you that manifest what you want. In addition, always bring a moment of slow motion into your routines. Look for ways for the body and mind to FEEL the emotions of the components in the LOVE energies.

Component Six: Follow a program to ascend and increase vibrations

The more of the LOVE energies you bring into your life, the more you move into higher spiritual capabilities of your body and mind. You will also enter further into the Inner World where the imaginary world and the Universal Mind/intelligence open up and it becomes easier to manifest things in the Outer World. You will begin to develop capabilities that you do not believe you have. Get rid of false beliefs and know you have the power to manifest anything. Work to delete your supposedly harmless statements like "*I hate…*", "*I am not feeling good*", "*I am sick of…*", "*That really pisses me off*", "*I can't stand it*", and the likes from your negative inventory of expressions. They do not serve you well. They are lethal energies. Always look for ways to do good, feel compassion and serve others to create a better life. A smile, a hand up, a few coins, perhaps things you have learned here. Charity, when "*given from the heart*" pays back ten fold. Always place forgiveness in your perception of any experience you have had, or are having. Look for things to forgive. Know there is no wrong or right so do not judge. Show compassion without judgment. If you feel any anxiety, guilt or fear, look to the root cause and forgive that which caused it. Forgive yourself. Look for ways that can accelerate your ascension and vibrations.

Component Seven: Solve issues and develop your ability to synchronize thought, feelings and emotion

This can be done before bed time in the horizontal position as part of going into lower brain waves in your sleep state. When you are in your bed and comfortable breathe slowly and deeply focusing on the quiet, peace and your breathing rhythm. It may take five minutes to bring the brain waves into Alpha, slowly eliminating everything else. There are two parts to this process when you are ready. First, it is a perfect time to raise questions for your mind to work on. As you breathe slowly and feel the peace of the Temple, bring your problems, issues or whatever, into the silent space at this time. Simply think the problem or even state it. Ask for help. Ask and listen for guidance about what to do. Ask for the answers to questions. Ask to be told what to do when in doubt. Be clear. Be patient and relaxed. You may find the answer comes later as a dream, thought, intuition, through someone or something else or another situation. You will not be able to determine when or how this will occur but you are creating energy packets that will eventually find their counterparts. Believe these will come. Once completed, relax and breathe softly and quietly as you charge your mind to start its work on its own.

Then begin a second process of being an actor. What you want to do is develop the ability of synchronizing thought, emotion and feeling. At the same time, you are going to synchronize and develop visualization and experience. Let me use an example of joy. Joy is an emotion. Everybody has a different body and mind experience with a joy. At first, think back to when you felt joy. Perhaps it is when your dog wags its tail really excited to see you. What was the feeling you had? Was it a tingle, goose bumps, warmness? What was the reaction of the body? Capture that and you can now generate an experience. Seeing the dog is your experience. It can be captured in a picture, a visualization where you see the dog, hug the dog, whatever generates the joy. So you create a thought *"there's my dog Sam"*, choose the emotion *"I feel joy"* and feel the consequence in your body. This could be warm feeling with goose bumps up your back. So practice these from memories until you get better. Then start to progress to a point where you can simply generate a thought and a picture and feel the emotions tingle through you as energy. Practice through a list for twenty minutes or until you fall asleep. Now, keep in mind that there is a hierarchy of power here in that the most powerful emotion that links to the center of the galaxy and the Divine center is an orgasm of two people united sexually in unconditional love. That is the ultimate communion with Spirit. I am not suggesting you do that here but it is a good alternative once in a while! You will certainly have a better appreciation for the energies! As we progress down the hierarchy we encounter love, love of others, compassion, gratitude, forgiveness, reverence, joy, harmony, blessing, and so on. These are highly potent emotions that are the language of Spirit that you can practice and enjoy before you sleep. The intensity of each is under your control but the stronger it is, the quicker it attracts. At any rate, you are going to move into the Inner World where you are One with Spirit and you are going to phase into a World of dreams and limitless possibilities – sleep.

THE NEW ALIGNMENT

You will find that if you follow a daily routine of directing the orchestra, incorporating the Spirit, Body and Mind codes, you will dramatically change the balance of negative-positive things in your life. As you pay attention to Spirit's Prime Purpose and your thoughts, get your body and mind tuned up, you build a resilience that quickly converts negative to positive. You will naturally head towards a more love-based existence that puts positive spin in everything you do, think, want and react on. You will begin to look for challenges from experiences that you were previously afraid of. Life will become a patchwork of fantastic adventures, experiences, and good emotions, regardless of what you encounter. Your trinity will respond. You will find that you will be attracting more positive energy in the form of people, events, and opportunities. They will simply begin to "appear" from nowhere. You will also be transmitting more positive energies and you will be training your energy systems to generate positive energies while on autopilot. You will be training the Ego to take orders from the heart. It will eventually begin to snowball for you.

This transcends automatically towards your objective of always having "high spirits." That does not mean drinking the stuff! You will notice that your Spirit, once it is fed a steady proper diet as in the Body and Mind Codes will simply begin to ascend you automatically. People will feel it and see it in you. Your heart center will expand its radius of influence and it will be immediately "felt" by others. That is simply the way it is. At the same time, you will be coming closer and closer to your Divine Self as meditation is the gateway to the Inner World. This is where you will be getting in touch with Spirit and INVOKING some capabilities that are already in you. You will begin to realize the boundless realm of possibilities in the Inner World are not limited to our material world.

But you must take the first step, give intent and DO IT! This is referred to as becoming a 4D human.

What you are going to implement with this Life Code is a plan for a new life. That means you can start creating a better life RIGHT NOW and it can only get better and better. It will get better beyond your comprehension. This Life Code will insure that your current limited comprehension, and limited physical state, does not inhibit what you can really do. Remember it takes a steady horse to run a long race!

IS THERE A MASTERS LEVEL?

There is a Masters level. But it does not require a Master to train you. You train yourself and the results are directly proportional to the effort you put into the Body, Mind and Spirit codes. The Masters level includes healing — miracles. By now you have no doubt heard about an unexplainable "miracle" in healing. There have been enough cases to substantiate the reality of them and the scientific world acknowledges them, the religious world has always had them and the ancient world founded them. If you are stuck on disbelief here then unstick yourself because it is real. So if you want to be a healer then put this in your program as the experience you want out of life.

But there is a way of making this happen faster. There is a common denominator here and it involves someone who truly believes in the Divine, walks the talk of love, compassion and forgiveness and is a genuine loving human working away at making the world a better place. The common denominator is also that the mode of prayer is used as the connection to the source that creates the miracle (Creator) and the healer is simply the facilitator to open the healing floodgate of energy. Healing requires blessing. Healing requires building the oneness with the Creator — and obviously a belief in One. Healing requires forgiveness. This means transcending judgment, and evaluation. Forgiveness is trust — in the Creator — in your intuition. Judgment inhibits the flow of love and healing energy does not survive. Now I speak of Divine healing and not other forms where the healer acts as a facilitator to help the person heal themselves. I mean real healing like wham, bamm, zap, it's done!

So here is an exercise for you. It is a test to see how well you can *walk the talk.* It should actually be *walk the thought.* As you know, emotion is THE key communication language because you can't fake it. So here is your test to see if you can create your first miracle. Look into your own life experience and find someone who did a very, bad, rotten thing to you. You have never forgotten this issue that was created. It cut deep in you. Now sit down in a quiet personal space, get quiet and BLESS and FORGIVE this person. Remember that the blessing is a potent process that MUST by definition incorporate the feelings of forgiveness, compassion and love. A blessing does not condone, it simply acknowledges an event and opens the heart to the victim, perpetrator and spectator. It is beyond judgment.

So think about this person and bless them several times. BLESS the person and BLESS yourself. If there were others involved, BLESS them too. State, think and visualize (if you can) the blessing over and over until you feel warmth of love build in your abdomen. Then feel the emotional energy rise and well up in your heart area to feel a *"pain of sorrow in the heart."* The next stage creates a constriction or choking in the throat as the compassion rises — like before you cry. Then as the energy rises to your head, you form tears in your eyes as they well up from the emotional release. You may even cry. Sit there, breath deeply and feel the new energy give peacefulness as it flows out to that person. You have brought energy up through your higher chakras and activated their spiritual parts.

If you can do this, you pass the test. You have created your first miracle because you completely re-wrote a part of your history and all the bad energy that surrounded this for whatever time is applicable simply does not exist. It vaporized into nothing and was replaced by the energy of love. You did a time flip to a good movie and at the same time purged old bad stuff — wham bam zap it's done! The bad frames are gone — don't exist in your mind. There is something else here. Let us suppose that you now choose to contact this person and meet, shake hands, hug and you both feel the emotion of joy and forgiveness. Guess what you have done? You have now flipped into the future script which is also totally different from the way the movie was going to be played out. You could have predicted that the script going forward would most likely continue to harbor negative energy and that the issue would not be resolved. There would be no frames in your movie involving this wretched person. But wham bam zap, not so! You created a miracle! So if you passed this test, what else can you do to change time? This, and living the LIFE CODE in this book IS the path to miracles.

SOME FINAL THOUGHTS

Now, I want to leave you with some final thoughts. Behind the Life Code and the Subtle Laws is a rationalization process that has pulled out common beliefs, facts, and findings from science, religion, ancient writings, prophesies, esoteric practices, and the New Age belief system. They all point to there being a "Creator" and that we are all One Family interconnected with the same prime purpose. Although I have not referenced any backup material, there is a surprising amount of research now available that confirms the existence of a force or "God" and that we are all a holographic part of creation. Scientists are changing their ideas about time and how we can indeed influence global and local changes with thought, emotion and feelings. They have come to conclusions that all of this dark space or "nothing" is actually an intelligent force that we can communicate with. Science is validating that we are changing — our DNA, our vibrations, our consciousness. Science is verifying that the esoteric sciences are not so silly after all. What I want to point out is this. The laws that I have listed were known to ancient civilizations and they are not new. These have been hidden from us but we are truly now discovering who and what we are, and what powers we have. It is not a silly joke any more. We can move with this new knowledge and reap what we sow in a totally different way — if we choose.

Is there a message here? Yes. By now it should be loud and clear. If you want to solve the world conflicts, solve yours first. The world situation of war, conflict and differences are a composite reflection of our individual beliefs. We all have a contribution to the mass consciousness that affects us by reflecting all that combined energy back. In what is presented in this book you should be able to see a common denominator of peace, love, harmony and abundance for all on the planet. All of the differences that we fight and conflict about with regards to economics, race and religion, you name it, totally obliterate the common philosophy of love and peace — the supposed foundation of all these belief systems. The fact is that at the root each has a valuable contribution towards a planetary unity of quality time for all. But we have gotten off that track because we reflect a duality and conflict — just being dumb Ego based humans. Are we not all striving to have a good, peaceful life? Make one yourself! Then help others that are not as fortunate as you make theirs. Are we really different and is that difference big enough to get angry, kill and fight about? We are all part of one big Intelligence. If so, *where is our* intelligence hidden?

There is an interesting Buddhist teaching: *"Enemies are as limitless as space; they cannot be overcome. Instead, overcome the hatred in your heart and there will be no more enemies."*

I want to leave one final message. In my research on miracles I ran across many documented cases of amazing miracles that were beyond medical or scientific comprehension. I found the characteristics of the people who had an amazing healing miracle happen to them very interesting. In one particular book, I read about many documented cases in the American Western Native culture, written by a medical doctor and miracle "facilitator." He noted that there were common characteristics clearly evident before and after a healing miracle (when there were no other alternatives) took place. Here they are:

Before the miracle happened, the patients had a strong internal focus of control for healing which included the following:

- An accurate appraisal of the problem and its threat
- A belief in self as agent for the healing
- A belief in personal change being needed

- A belief in healing being possible
- A belief in a personal capacity to heal through faith
- A sense of self-empowerment

With regards to life's meaning, the patients showed a common belief system including the following:

- Our lives and suffering have purpose (family, God, love)
- They had a plan and projects for future despite fatal sickness
- They refused to give up and die
- A continued life would result in increase in fulfillment
- Life's purpose was to help and benefit others
- A sense of joy would accompany fulfilling life's purpose

Upon having a healing miracle occur, the patients underwent a personal transformation which included the following:

- Changes in personality
- Ability to identify feelings better
- Ability to express feelings better
- Identification with new self image
- A sense of new values and valuation of life

Upon completing the healing miracle, patients underwent a Spiritual transformation (on healing journey) as follows:

- Change in sense of unity and connection with all things
- Sense of presence of a higher power
- Increase in importance of spirituality in guiding one's life
- Increase in feeling life is directed by spiritual principles
- Increase in sense of peacefulness
- A sense of surrender of what cannot be changed
- Acceptance of all possibilities including death

After the miracle, in looking at the patient's quality of life, the healing effectively impacted the following ways:

- Increased emotional well being
- Ability to tolerate and manage distressing emotions
- Increased comfort and enjoyment of physical body
- Feelings of self-worth and life satisfaction
- Sense of being on path of life's purpose
- Increased pleasure/joy/laughter

After the miracle, the patients experienced a heightened sense of value in relationships. These were as follows:

- Increased experience of intimacy
- Pleasure and joy in relationships
- Sense of being nonjudgmental
- Increased forgiveness as they released hurt and anger
- Letting go of the future instead of trying to control it
- Expanded degree of relationships
- More ability to love
- Improved family relationships

After the healing, the patients exhibited a new mindset desire to transform their lives to something new:

- Need to make a change
- Ability to take action on a change
- Willingness to initiate action on changes
- Applying self diligently to make a change

I have to state that these characteristics are common to miracles documented in medical science, western religions, native cultures, eastern religions, the bible, esoteric/occult practices, and near death experiences. Does this sound familiar? Does this have any resemblance to the Secret Subtle Laws and the Codes? Is there a message here? Yes, why die or wait until your life is at risk to learn the above characteristics for a quality life? Why not make some simple choices and do it NOW with the Spirit, Body and Mind Code? Then the rest of your life will indeed be a miracle.

That is my HEART TO HEART TALK!
Have a wonderful life!

Ed Rychkun

BOOK ABSTRACTS BY Ed Rychkun
www.edrychkun.com

The Secret Little Book: A New Age Prescription for a Great Life In this short little book, Ed Rychkun reveals what it has taken him "many lifetimes" to learn. He lays out a simple "down to earth" bottom line summary of the New Age. He then reveals his powerful secrets to a complete Body, Mind and Spirit Prescription for health and prosperity. In a simple, easy to read format, he summarizes his 8 Secret Truths of the Universe that have a direct affect on how you manifest a joyful life of abundance, harmony and love. Ed unfolds a simple Life Plan for everyone, then takes you on a quick journey of ascension and the New Age Great Awakening of 2012. This stunning Book will prepare you for a dynamic new future unfolding on this planet. ***Take the New Age Prescription for a great life.***

The Book of Secrets: Breaking the Chains of your Spiritual and Commercial Bondage. In this book, Ed Rychkun tells a story about two happy Light Beings who volunteered for a special mission to planet Earth. Having been incarnated as Tom and Pam Doubtfull, they have been captured in a commercial and spiritual illusion that has consumed their existence. Live with them as they meet two Mentors and uncover the Secrets about the Cloak of the Matrix and how the truth has been hidden from them by the Global Elite. See how they cast away the old belief system to unplug from this Matrix. Learn the secrets of how they break their chains of Spiritual and Commercial bondage to walk through a new door into a new reality, and their New Age birthright. Learn how they *Wake up and unplug from the Spiritual and Commercial Illusion.*

Subtle Secrets: Talking Heart to Heart If you have ever had moments where you pondered why your life has unfolded the way it has and whether you had any control over making it better, you need to read this profound summary that combines ancient wisdom with recent scientific discoveries. In this book, Ed Rychkun gets to the "Heart" of how to manifest a life of quality time providing concise riveting information about why you need to start paying attention to the Subtle Laws of the Universe. These Subtle Laws reveal the common purpose of life transcending the boundaries of race and religious and spiritual differences so common on our conflictive planet. From the ancient wisdom of the ages, to the miracle healings of the religions, through New Age beliefs and from the most recent scientific discoveries, Ed extracts the essence of a common purpose and process with a resounding message: *"If you want to heal the planet, and generate love and peace, start with yourself and your own back yard. Then direct your mind to change your code of behavior to create coherence between the two main subtle energy centers - the heart and brain".* Take the action to manifest a quality life and activate your role to a peaceful planet.

The Book of Secrets: Taking Back Your Financial and Spiritual Powers In this revealing book, Ed Rychkun continues the journey out of the Commercial and Spiritual Matrix imposed by the Global Elite. Learn astonishing secrets as Tom and Pam Doubtfull, two descended Light Beings who have now awakened from the deception of the Cloak of the Matrix, continue to dig deeper and deeper into the truth behind the Commercial and Spiritual Illusion. Learn how they create a Commercial Duality and recover the powers they have lost. In a compelling dialogue, Tom is subjected to the Commercial Martial Arts to earn his belts, each time opening a new door towards financial freedom. Here he uncovers new tactical secrets in the hidden private world of commerce to develop an arsenal of secret unpublished financial offensive and defensive weapons. See also how they transmute themselves spiritually by rejecting their Religious Duality to ultimately develop their new life plan leading them on their new journey towards ascension. *Learn to take back your own financial and spiritual powers.*

Shift Happened: The Ubiquitology Handbook to the Peak Living Zone Take an exciting new journey into the new shift revolutionalizing health care in this provocative handbook on Ubiquitology – healing by connecting mind and body with Spirit. Ronald Conn, a popular radio personality, and Founder of Ubiquity Wellness Centre, North America's foremost private preventative, natural wellness clinic, reveals how after his Near Death Experience he gave birth to his vision and has used revolutionary Ubiquitous healing methods to help thousands achieve their health and wellness goals. Learn how to stay in the Peak Living Zone as Ed Rychkun, former business executive, Reiki Master and Spiritual Writer takes you to the bottom line of how the Subtle Laws of the Universe work. He tells you why your life is the way it is, and how, by paying attention to the laws of subtle energies, manifesting a better quality life can become a reality. Together, Ronald and Ed provide a mind blowing handbook taking you onto the fast-track to optimum health and quality life through their simple Mind, Body and Spirit Code. *Take the action to get into the Peak Living Zone.*

Commercial Martial Arts I: Taking off the Cloak of the Illuminati Matrix. In this work of fiction, Ed Rychkun explains how the Illuminati have captured Tom, a typical businessman, into their herd of Sheeple. He, like Nations, have unknowingly accepted the invisible Cloak of the Matrix that makes them and him a human capital machine working for a Strawman. Being siphoned by the commercial deception and fed the illusion of freedom, it is time for Tom to wake up. Understanding how bankrupt Nations have bonded him into paying for their folly, he wakes up to how this global deception has been implemented by the Global Elite. Watch as he takes off the Cloak and prepares himself for the Commercial Martial Arts. Learn the obscured, hidden secrets as Tom's Mentor leads him into the power of the Private World of Commerce, and how the Commercial and Spiritual Illusion can work for him. *Understand the Deception and take back your Private Freedoms.*

Commercial Martial Arts II: Taking Back Your Financial Powers In this work of fiction, Ed Rychkun takes you on a profound new journey through the commercial illusion. With the Cloak of the Matrix taken off, Tom is now able to learn his offensive and defensive weapons to take back his financial powers. As Tom's Mentor takes him through his Martial Arts lessons, he learns how to make the Strawman work for him and how to structure his financial affairs in the Private world of commerce. Through Tom's lessons, he learns how he can unplug from the legal, tax and banking siphons to take back his financial powers. Tom's tactical, unpublished secrets of deploying his new path towards Preparing, Privatizing and Protecting his financial world, changes his life forever. *Bring the power of the private world of Commerce into your reality.*

The Book of Secrets: Preparing For Ascension In this book, Ed Rychkun continues the journey of ascension with Tom and Pam Doubtfull, two descended Light Beings who have awoken to who they really are. Having discovered how they have been captured into the commercial and spiritual illusions, they now know exactly how to unplug from the Cloak of the Matrix and take back their spiritual and financial powers. Now Tom and Pam must set a practical new course that takes them through a Life Plan and back to their lineage of Spirit – their birthright. Follow Pam and Tom as they now lay out their steps of ascending from their 3D material conundrum into 4D and 5D light beings, crossing over the 2012 zero point predicted by the Mayans. Learn how they rationalize the conflicting prophesies, galactic cataclysms, Earth upheaval, and economic collapse using New Age, scientific, biblical and esoteric evidence to determine their ultimate plan. Follow them in their struggle to go back to Nature, leave the material world behind and prepare for their final homecoming. *Prepare yourself for Ascension and the Great Awakening.*

You Are Fired Said the Heart to the Ego In this unusual and profound book, Ed Rychkun takes you to a critical situation that occurs between a human's heartbeats. In a last ditch effort to make sure the next beat occurs, the Heart engages in a desperate conversation with the Ego whom it blames for the demise of the human. In a fascinating dialogue between the Heart, the Ego, the Brain, the Mind, the Soul, the Chakra Children, and God, Ed takes you to the split second where time ceases and the physical material world becomes one with the Spiritual and Subtle energy counterparts. Learn how the Ego has taken the command center away from the sleeping Mind making the Brain, Soul, Heart, and Chakra Children subservient players in directing the quality of human life. Learn how the crisis deadlock is broken and the decision is made whether the next heartbeat is allowed to occur. See if you can deduct the same conclusions and reject or accept a coherent harmony between the six characters that control the human's life. *Will you Fire the Ego and put the power back where it belongs?*

Rychkun's Laws of AQ'ISM Want a fresh, new humorous look at the business world we all live in? Take a tour of corporate life through Ed Rychkun's view of his lifetime of climbing corporate ladders. This provocative and hilarious expose' shows what really goes on behind those boardroom walls. It reveals the flip side of a company's naked underbelly by showing how people universally conform to laws on how they feel about each other called AQ'ISM – a classification of "Asshole". Ed examines the social behavior of corporate citizens and develops his universal laws about how this feeling is quantified as an AQ, and how it can have a direct impact on how fast you can climb or fall from the corporate ladder. Ed tells it like it is, revealing how the "real" professionals - the Executives, use a set of secret AQ Arsenals to hide their incompetence - and maintain their positions of power in the corporate hierarchy. You will immediately recognize a similarity with your own situation and derive humor from it. But beware... as one critic points out, *"Never was the raw naked truth so aptly expressed as in this earthy examination of the blatantly exposed underbelly of the modern corporation". Learn how to avoid being a Corporate Asshole!*

Who Said Fishing Was Serious? Here is the best fishing and fireside companion you could ask for. This book is full of short fishing stories that started out serious but turned into funny, gut-wrenching calamities. You will be amazed at the crazy situations that Ed has selected. Focusing on stories that pit the large brained angler against that small pea-brained fish, Ed will have you in stitches as he and his brother take to the challenge. See if you can contain yourself when you read the events that unfold in his short stories. How many times has your own technical assault on those little fish turned into a side-splitting laughing frenzy? Checkout Ed's special selection of not so serious fishing mis-adventures taken from his many years of fishing for that BIG ONE. Who Said Fishing Was Serious? is a refreshing experience into laughter. See if you can contain yours. *See how serious you take fishing after indulging in these stories.*

Xolani and the Magic Shanty In this Adult/Children's book, Ed Rychkun tells the story of Xolani, an angry 12 year old Zulu boy living in Shanty Town in South Africa. Life is not good here and he has taken up with a band of ruffians to get back at the wealthy and the Whites whom they have learned to hate. One day Xolani finds a Magic Shanty and meets and unusual Nharo Medicine Man. Xolani finds he is not as bad as he thought and some of his Crystal Child characteristics are making life a conflict. Suddenly life begins to change for him and the people around him as he begins to blossom, and he learns how he can make his own Magic Shanty. Follow his life changing experience in the poverty stricken Shanty Town as he changes his and everyone else's life. Shanty Town will never be the same. *Live with Xolani as he unfolds his new destiny*

A Private Limited Liability Enterprise

www.edrychkun.com

Made in the USA
Monee, IL
08 July 2026

56712988R00049